T0161125

# GOD'S CHOSEN Leader

## A MAN AFTER GOD'S HEART

APOSTLE (DR.) EMMANUEL NUHU KURE

# GOD'S CHOSEN LEADER

©2021 by Dr. Emmanuel Nuhu Kure     **First Edition** 1998
**ISBN:** 978-1-952025-61-7     **Second Edition** 2021

**Published by** Carpenter's Son Publishing, Franklin, TN
**Published in association with** Larry Carpenter of Christian Book Services, LLC    **www.christianbookservices.com**

**Scriptures are taken from** the KING JAMES VERSION (KJV): KING JAMES VERSION, public domain.
**Edited by** Dr. William Combs and Judy Combs
**Cover Design by** Suzanne Lawing
**Interior Design by** Dr. William Combs

**Forward all inquiries to:**
Throneroom (Trust) Ministry, Inc.
Zion International Prayer and Retreat Camp
Throneroom Close, Off Hospital Road
PO Box 266, Kafanchan, Kaduna State, Nigeria.
Tel. Nigeria: +234-8051817164 / US: +1-850-559-0024

Printed in the United States of America

# CONTENTS

# DEDICATION

Dedicated to those who like me, cry to be clothed always with His Glory in Ministry: the Rapture Generation of Ministers, and to the only closest minister friend whose void has proved difficult to fill in my life, and whose transparent life, raw passion for God and His callings, transcends any I have ever seen in any minister (high and low) in Nigeria. He gave me back my sanity by his life and passion in our barely three-year fellowship of the last part of his pilgrimage on earth, when I felt I was the odd one out and was giving up on the church. The man who, knowing it was his last week sent a courier to me in the north of Nigeria to come quickly that we might enter the presence of the Lord together for a last time to inquire of Him and commune with Him about his going and program. A man who wished for a second chance to affect a generation with the wholeness of God and bring complete glory to the church. He was carried in chariots of fire surrounded by elders in heaven crying for more of the ONE whom he loved. He descried this himself as he went. To Rev. (Dr.) I. K. EBENEME, Faith Clinic International Ibadan, and to the ONE we loved together most – the MOST HIGH GOD and His Son JESUS CHRIST do I dedicate this book.

# PREFACE

The need to clear many basic things in scripture about God's anointed vessels of honor that have been called to bear his oils has always hunted me. I have seen a lot of ministers rise and fall. I have seen a lot seeming contradictions in ministers and the way ministries are run. A lot of people, especially the younger generation do not understand any more what ministry is all about. Ministers and ministries are losing focus and the church of God is restless. If this trend is allowed to continue, the church will soon not be able to tell why it exists, and ministers will not be able to tell why they are ministers or whether the sacrifice is worth it or not. Already, many young men in ministry go in for subsistence purposes, or for the glitter in it especially where they are Pentecostals.

These are voids I have grappled with in life as a minister, for which God revealed Himself and filled; voids and hunger which every minister grapples with. I saw the Lord going from house to house in the spirit raising fresh men to restore the glory of the Church, and the focus that will bring Jesus back. He gave them a proper direction the church should follow. It was in the midst of the changes He was carrying out in the church that He commissioned me to write this word (book), for those who like me, cry for His glory in everything and would settle for nothing less.

As you read this book, you are expected to pause from place to place, to commune with the Master in your heart, rendering prayer about conforming to His image in ministry that an oil and a generation might be born through you and these words of the Lord.

# ACKNOWLEDGMENTS

I wish to bless the men and women in the wings of God's spiritual move who have made this book possible. – Pastor Joseph Kyari, Mrs. Naomi Aruwa and Bro. Omofuma Felix (Shell, Warri). The Lord make you a memorial for Himself.

Glory to God for Bill and Judy Combs who facilitated the printing in the US and contributed to its production.

Thanks to Larry Carpenter for publishing this edition in the United States.

When the Malachi 3:10 records are written, it shall be recorded that, by your sacrifices, the Church received life.

God bless you,
Kure

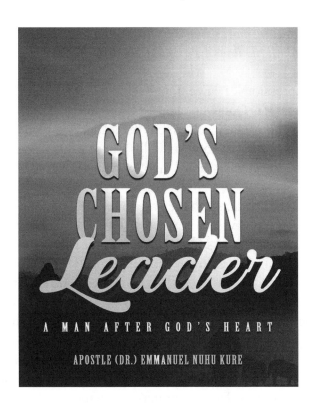

# CHAPTER
# 1

# I Have Found David My Servant

*"I have found David my servant; with my holy oil have I anointed him: With whom my hand shall be established: mine arm also shall strengthen him. The enemy shall not exact upon him; nor the son of wickedness afflict him. And I will beat down his foes before his face, and plague them that hate him. But my faithfulness*

*and my mercy shall be with him: and in my name shall his horn be exalted"* (Psalm 89:20 - 24).

The expression "I have found David my servant," clearly shows that it is God who chooses every leader. There are leaders who choose themselves, but the leader that God finds and lifts up is promoted above all odds. He sets that leader against odds and the gates of hell cannot prevail against that leader.

Leaders are servants and they are found by God. The question you must ask yourself is whether God has found you. God finds His leaders; His leaders cannot find Him. God chooses his elders, his elders do not choose themselves. You may want to submit and avail yourself in one area, but God may not choose to use you in the area you avail yourself. God does not choose a leader until he has something in mind. When God chooses you, then he has something up his sleeve. He wants to release you to change your life and to do something for Him. If you find yourself in a leadership position, it means there is an oil to offer. Do not go making mistakes, else the work will die and the oil will dry up. There is an oil to offer; your business is to find the oil. God said, "David my servant have I found and with my anointing oil have I anointed him."

It is not by mistake that the Lord puts you in a place of leadership. It means there is a hidden oil for that leadership. Do not allow that ministry to die because if it does, your spiritual life will die too. It does not matter where you are; whether in the Church or house fellowship. If you are a president, there is an oil in you to change the people you are leading. If you are a pastor, or a head of a ministry, there is hidden oil; otherwise, God has not found you. Get out of that place. God does not want you in that position.

Some years back, a brother was approached by his local assembly to become a pastor. He replied, "Thus saith the Lord, I should not be made pastor, my hour has not yet come." After two years, they came back and said, "We want to ordain you a pastor." He still refused. Meanwhile, he was affecting lives in his city, doing even pastoral work. He was a prayer warrior. When they came again that year he said to me, "Brother Kure, the Lord seemed to be saying SUBMIT." I told him go ahead and obey God because the hour for him to carry the mantle had come.

Timing is important, the place is important. If they had anointed him before, they would have anointed him into the wrong place. Now that the hour had come and he went to take his oil, the oil will find a meaningful place. God does not anoint you with oil except there is a place for it. The oil is meant to carry out a purpose.

**YOU ARE CHOSEN FOR A PURPOSE**
*"Ye have not chosen me, but I have chosen you, and ordained you, that ye should go and bring forth fruit, and that your fruit should remain: that whatsoever ye shall ask of the Father in my name, he may give it you"* (John 15:16)

If you find yourself as a leader, then you can change the people around you. There is a purpose for your oil. You can change your city and turn it around. If God chooses you, then there is an oil in you to make the land and the people fertile and fruitful in order to make the people see light. God will set you on fire to change destinies. Otherwise, God has not found you. It is the oil that proclaims the vision of God, it is the oil.

**Thus saith the Spirit of the Lord, "If you shall break the walls of your own planning abilities and wisdom in approaching the**

work of the Lord, the mysteries of the land shall bow at your feet, yea the riches of the land shall be brought forth unto your feet. Yea, the strongest shall carry you on their shoulders and it shall come to pass that by you, territories, strange and new, shall be broken. I see you as a ruler of the land. I see you as one that carries the oil. I see you as one that pours oil that cannot be resisted. I see great signs, I see the dead rise. It shall come to pass that a violence shall come upon your spirit and the oil of that violence shall break the grounds that many men have not been able to break for many centuries. In that day, ye shall not remember that you have a name, as men remember your name. As men begin to call your name, pride shall not come in. You shall be careful not to rule over men but rule after the Spirit. You shall do only that which the Spirit of the Lord puts into you to do. Then your life shall be fulfilled."

There are leaders who made themselves and there are leaders God made. The problem we have in the church today is with the leaders who have made themselves, not those whom God called. These self-made leaders have neither purpose nor direction. They mix up the oils for other people who are called. They stand in the way. They want to take the mantle of those who have purpose, and those who have clear directions. They want to copy those who are called. Where they do not succeed in copying, they cause problems by telling lies, doing all kinds of terrible things just to bring down the "called." Their motive is: since they cannot make it, nobody else should. They forget that He who dwells in the Highest must pass through a way, and when he decides to pass through a way, anyone that stands before him, he shall be trampled upon.

**Let me tell you, the oil God puts upon your head is to make God pass through a way, and anybody who stands in the way, through which God will pass, God will trample upon that person.**

A leader who is not called by God has a tragic end because he is bound to make terrible mistakes. Saul was not chosen by God to rule Israel. His appointment was in response to the stubborn request by Israel – Hitherto Israel was ruled by priests and prophets, people who could hear from God and carry out His bidding to the letter. But Israel preferred to have a king over them.

> *"Nevertheless the people refused to obey the voice of Samuel; and they said, Nay; but we will have a king over us; That we also may be like all the nations; and that our king may judge us, and go out before us, and fight our battles."*
> (1 Samuel 8:19 – 20)

The children of Israel chose to rebel against God in spite of wise counsel from Samuel. They had soon forgotten that prior to this time Samuel had led them to battle successfully because he always received instructions from God. The battle is the Lord's. They just wanted to imitate other nations. God in His infinite mercy still forgave Israel as a nation.

> *"And Samuel said unto the people, Fear not: ye have done all this wickedness: yet turn not aside from following the Lord, but serve the Lord with all your heart; And turn ye not aside: for then should ye go after vain things, which*

*cannot profit nor deliver; for they are vain. For
the Lord will not forsake his people for his great
name's sake: because it hath pleased the Lord
to make you his people."*
(1 Samuel 12:20 – 22)

No sooner had Saul been made king than he began to rumble, he began to make gruesome mistakes. This is a characteristic of a self-made ruler. He degenerated from perpetual disobedience, attempted murder to divination.

The climax of Saul's fall was when in 1 Samuel 15, he spared Agag the king of the Amalekites along with the best of the sheep, and oxen, the rattling and the lambs. He argued that the spoils he kept were meant to sacrifice unto the Lord God in Gilgal. How could God contradict himself? The commandment of God was that Saul should utterly destroy the Amalekites and their property. This act of disobedience broke God's heart so much that God regretted making Saul a king.

*"Then came the word of the Lord unto Samuel,
saying, It repenteth me that I have set up Saul
to be king: for he is turned back from following me, and hath not performed my command-
ments. And it grieved Samuel; and he cried
unto the Lord all night"* (1 Samuel 15:10 – 11).

There are grounds to be broken. I do not believe that any ground that hears the oil of the Lord will refuse to open up. With God all things are possible. I know it, all things are possible in your flesh, in your life. All we need is ask the father to take away that nature that resists him, and to enforce the law of his Spirit in the midst of the earth. God is a Spirit and by His Spirit the earth shall prosper.

God does not give an oil without a purpose. If you are ordained and up till how you do not know the purpose for your ordination, then you need to go back for a long retreat and wrestle with God. Tell him, "Father, if I am not called by you, then call me now." If man ordained you and you do not understand the purpose of your ordination, it is time to go and battle with God. He can still give you a purpose. But I tell you, except there is a purpose, there cannot be an oil for it. It is the purpose and vision that guides the person and leads him by the hand. The oil is the embodiment of the vision. And the vision is the purpose that God wants you to carry out, not your own purpose.

There is a popular scripture that we have in our ministry. It is found in John 4:34 *"My meat is to do the will of him that sent me, and to finish his work."* This is Jesus talking now. He is telling you the focus of His oil.

Note one thing: God gets everyone born-again. But he does not get everybody anointed. It is not everybody that God releases to carry a mantle, no matter how small the task. The purpose is in different dimensions. It could be very small just doing it in your own small way, and it could be very big for nations. It could be in a very specialized direction. But God has never made a man a jack of all trades. Anyone who tells you that he is an apostle of all trades is a liar. Jesus was anointed to cast out demons, made the raging sea calm, healed the sick. But the purpose of His anointing was to go to the cross and defeat Satan in hell and redeem man's lost glory.

The casting out of demons was to clear the way for the purpose to be fulfilled. When God anoints you, everything you do on the way: casting out demons, bringing people into the church eventually, is to fulfill the main thing for which you are called. Jesus had one focus in his anointing: to bring about rebirth in mankind and there is no way he could bring rebirth without casting out demons. Bringing salvation to mankind was the purpose for his anointing. That is why the book of Acts 10:38 says,

> *"How God anointed Jesus of Nazareth with the Holy Ghost and with power: who went about doing good, and healing all that were oppressed of the devil; for God was with him. And we are witnesses of all things which he did both in the land of the Jews, and in Jerusalem."*

He went about. He was on a mission doing good and healing all who were oppressed of the devil for God was with him. It was the clear sense of direction that Jesus had that made him to say in John 4:34, "My meat," that is the only thing that satisfies my spirit, the only reason why I am alive, the only thing that will give me joy, "is to do the will of him that sent me." That means the purpose of your being sent here is to do the will of the father.

There is no leadership without a purpose, and the purpose does not come from the person; it comes from heaven. It is not manufactured by the leader. Some people are busy planning out programs for their ministry. They sit to draw out plans; things they want to accomplish for God. Each time, they do that saying that Jesus left them the ministry of reconciliation, therefore, they are going to reconcile people, they are appointing themselves. There is no doubt that Jesus left us the ministry of reconciliation.

However, there is a portion of that ministry that is the main goal of Jesus for your life. There is a part for you, you cannot be a jack of all trades. What you need to do is to find out the exact thing you have been assigned to do, that is your main focus. I know mine is to make nations bow; to turn around nations to fulfill prophecies and loosen the way for the King to come. I am anointed to break everything that stands in my way as I walk towards that purpose for nations. If a nation stands in the way, I will break the boundaries of that nation. It has to fall. If demons stand in the way, the ground will open up and they shall be buried inside. Anybody who stood in the way of Moses was punished. When the Israelites stood against Moses and said they were going back to Egypt, God said, "Since I said Canaan, but you are saying Egypt, let the ground open and all who wish to return to Egypt be swallowed." A second time they attempted, and God said, "you will not go to Egypt, but perish in the wilderness. They were led to Canaan, that was the purpose of God. It had the oil, and He ensured that the purpose was fulfilled even if the whole earth had to be given up. If God has to give up a thousand men to make your oil fulfill, a thousand men will die, they will be bulldozed out of the way.

> *"For I am the Lord thy God, the Holy One of Israel, thy Saviour: I gave Egypt for thy ransom, Ethiopia and Seba for thee. Since thou wast precious in my sight, thou hast been honourable, and I have loved thee: therefore will I give men for thee, and people for thy life."*
> (Isaiah 43:3 – 4)

Alas, if you have been ordained to spread the gospel, make life difficult for the devil because God has set you as a watchman to take the earth: to prepare it and open it up so that His glory can dwell inside and God can set His throne and rule freely. Therefore, anything that stands in the way has to die. It has to be uprooted. You can make all the difference if you are the right leader. You can make all the difference in your territory, your church, etc.

# FUNCTIONS OF A PRIEST OR LEADER
## READ EZEKIEL 34:1 – 31

Ezekiel 34:4 and Luke 4:18 - 19
1. To heal that which was sick.
    This includes Matthew 25:34 – 40;
2. To bind up that which was broken. Take care of loose ends in individual lives and in ministry;
3. To bring back those who were driven away;
4. To save the lost – harvest;
5. To preach deliverance to the captives;
6. Recovering of sight to the blind;
7. To set at liberty them that are bruised; and,
8. To preach the acceptable time/year of the Lord – preach fulfillment of prophecy.

Anything short of the above is cruelty on the part of the leader or priest and that will bring judgment on the priest or leader.

Any leader that cannot live up to the above practically should refuse leadership. A curse is on any leader or shepherd who would not do the above and would not allow those whose hearts are submitted and available to do it. The Bible says,
> *"Cursed be he that doeth the work of the Lord deceitfully, and cursed be he that keepeth back his sword from blood"* (Jeremiah 48:10).

If you cannot live up to the above and you insist on holding your post, you are robbing heaven of its expression and the flock of its glorification. You are cursed. You are an anti-Christ or you have an anti-Christ spirit. You should be cast out of the position.

Whether you are an apostle or a prophet or a pastor or an evangelist or a teacher, or you have all of the nine spiritual gifts, or you are talented with any kind of talent you use in the church including governance and helps, if they in their different approaches to the gospel do not fulfill all the points above, you have not entered into the fullness of ministry and fulfillment yet.

> *"And they were scattered, because there is no shepherd: and they became meat to all the beasts of the field, when they were scattered"* (Ezekiel 34:5).

The primary function of the shepherd is to being God to the people and when he is not doing that, the people become meat to the beasts of the field.

The minister's calling is not to get fat or get clothed while the people suffer. The people are the glory of the shepherd, not the garments they wear or the kind of car and house they live in, and where their children school. The people are our glory and crown. Clothe them and you shall be taken care of by heaven. Jesus did not only take care of his own *"those that thou gavest me I have kept, and none of them is lost"* for He healed Peter's mother-in-law, raised Lazarus (Mary's brother) from the dead, fed the crowd and stopped the storm from doing the disciples any harm. But He also came to seek the lost and to save them. Zacchaeus, disadvantaged in everything, physically and spiritually, dined with him because Jesus found him (Luke 19:1 – 9).

Jesus said to Paul,
> *"for I have appeared unto thee for this purpose, to make thee a minister and a witness both of these things which thou hast seen, and of those things in the which I will appear unto thee; Delivering thee from the people, and from the*

*Gentiles, unto whom now I send thee, To open their eyes, and to turn them from darkness to light, and from the power of Satan unto God, that they may receive forgiveness of sins, and inheritance among them which are sanctified by faith that is in me"* (Acts 26:16 – 18).

Paul's glorious testimony at the end in Acts 26:19,
> *"Whereupon, O king Agrippa, I was not disobedient unto the heavenly vision."*

He also said to Timothy,
> *"I have fought a good fight, I have finished my course, I have kept the faith: Henceforth there is laid up for me a crown of righteousness, which the Lord, the righteous judge, shall give me at that day: and not to me only, but unto all them also that love his appearing."*
>
> (2 Timothy 4:7 – 8)

The question you must ask yourself is not what are you, but who are you? Who have you in practice and reality been working for, Jesus or yourself? Is there a hope of glory in heaven at the end of your stewardship?

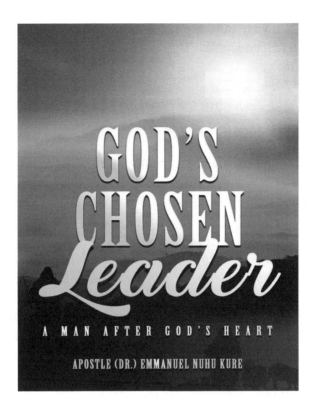

# CHAPTER 2

## The Oil Serves The Purpose

You see, it is the oil that expands itself, not man. I stay in this small town, Kafanchan, but I get invitations from all over the world. The oil does the calling, the oil serves the purpose for which it was sent. The oil has always served that purpose such that even Satan could not hold Jesus back.

The oil that ordained Jesus was meant to bring back man from chains to liberty. And the place of the chains of man was in death, in hell and hades. That is why the Bible says in Revelations 1:18,

> *"I am he that liveth, and was dead; and, behold, I am alive for evermore, Amen; and have the keys of hell and of death."*

He had to get to where the chains were. That is why if you want to break Satan, break the chains. You must learn to break chains and gates. You have the power because God gave you the keys to gates.

> *"And I say also unto thee, That thou art Peter, and upon this rock I will build my church; and the gates of hell shall not prevail against it. And I will give unto thee the keys of the kingdom of heaven: and whatsoever thou shalt bind on earth shall be bound in heaven: and whatsoever thou shalt loose on earth shall be loosed in heaven"* (Matthew 16:18 – 19).

Keys open gates. Since heaven and hell have keys, it means they both have gates and until Jesus broke through those gates to take the devil captive, His mission was not complete; and what empowered Jesus to do all these was the anointing. The anointing makes the difference. This is because the anointing is God. It is very vital for you to know that the anointing is God.

Have you ever stopped to ask why the mountain skipped like rams and ran away when they saw Israel and Jacob? It is because they saw God walking towards them in Israel.

> *"When Israel went out of Egypt, the house of Jacob from a people of strange language; Ju-*

*dah was his sanctuary, and Israel his domin-*
*ion. The sea saw it, and fled: Jordan was driven*
*back. The mountains skipped like rams, and the*
*little hills like lambs"* (Psalm 114:1 – 4).

The anointing is God. That is why the Bible says it is the anointing that breaks the yoke. If you have nothing, have the anointing.

If you are a pastor and you do not feel the compulsion in your spirit to do the work, resign or else you will not make it. Note, the anointing God gave you has power to gather both the people and the resources to do the work. The important thing is to understand how the principles of leadership operate in heaven. Gather leaders and teach them the mind of God concerning leadership so that men with direction shall emerge for God. The Joel army is being born from sets of leaders. They will be the vanguard to show others how to do it.

## A STEADY FLOW OF ANOINTING FROM GOD
How does a leader ensure a steady flow of anointing from God? First and foremost, he must maintain the right relationship with God. That gives him the assurance of his calling;:talking to God and God talking back to him. That is a great weapon.

I used to fear that I will not live long because I am too emotional about God. I talk to Him so often, so informally, that I can sit watching television at the same time talking to God. You can be talking to me while I am talking to God. I will not hear what you are saying because my concentration is on God. When you talk to God, be transparent. It is in your nakedness that God clothes you. You do not put on a rag and say, "God, I want clothes." He will not put clothes over a rag. Remove the rag, then the clothes will come. God will not give you the clothes when you are putting on a rag.

**Another major weapon is love.** Showing love in the place of bitterness is the strength of every leader. My greatest weakness is that I take friendship too seriously. Even when my friends are angry with me, I still visit them. Even when they spit into my eyes, I still visit them. That makes them want to trample more on me. It makes them feel too important. But it is the secret of my strength. That is how I have survived. So that in the day that a friend curses me, the curses will catch him because in the day of his repulsion it was love that answered. Love can swallow arrows. Some of you do not know that love can neutralize arrows. Love is a neutralizer. That is why God said love your enemies and pray for them that hate you.

> *"But I say unto you, Love your enemies, bless them that curse you, do good to them that hate you, and pray for them which despitefully use you, and persecute you; That ye may be the children of your Father which is in heaven: for he maketh his sun to rise on the evil and on the good, and sendeth rain on the just and on the unjust"* (Matthew 5:44 – 45).

Your love automatically becomes a shield. It swallows their arrows and makes them of no effect. Do not be angry. Keep loving your enemies even when they continue to trample upon you until the Lord says stop. There is a balance to it because there will be a point when the Lord will not want to expose you to their trampling anymore. At that time, if they dare to trample on you anymore, judgment will come upon them. Do not take the oil for granted.

But rest assured that God is the oil, and all things are possible with the oil. You need to look at your ministry or business and stretch your hand toward the ailing ministry or business and say, "God is the oil. Oh ministry, you cannot stop God. So, I push out of you that darkness, that poverty, the demon that is resisting me. Get out of here because God is the oil."

Begin to command the ministry or business to re-open. My friends, we need to get violent. You need to tell territorial spirits to get out. Let them know that God is the owner of the ground wherein their foundations are laid. Command them to give way. Use the keys of heaven to open up heaven for your ministry and take the keys of hell to release the captives. Always take the keys to open gates. It is relevant according to situations. If you look at the history of battles, chains, gates and doors are the major hindrances. Open them up and your life will open up. You are supposed to be the first fruit of success to show yourself and your members that is possible to succeed. When they see your example, they too will arise and do likewise.

## YOU HAVE NO RIGHT OF YOUR OWN
*"Jesus saith unto them, My meat is to do the will of him that sent me, and to finish his work"* (John 4:34).

Do you know what that means? It means the day you become a leader, you have no privacy. You have no will again. There are no more decisions to make but to seek His own will and decision, that you will succeed. Some people might wonder if one does not have one's own views. The day you have submitted to Him, you have lost that right. You have no right to any views anymore. This is not democracy. It is not the government that is in control. If you do not want to lose your right, get out of leadership. God will forgive you for disobeying Him and sometimes punish you at the end.

"My meat, my very existence is to do the will of God." This

means I cannot have my own way. It means that Jesus only rested when God allowed him to rest; and would not rest when God did not permit him. That is why you will notice that each time the cloud lifted up and moved, the Israelites had no right to rest; they had to move. They rested only when the cloud ceased to move.

The minister and leader must NOT throughout his life attract men to himself, but to Him that sent him. He must not make them rely on him but on the infallible and exhaustible provision of God's divine grace. He is always bringing people to Him and helping them know Him and making Him adopt them. This is his work all his life, helping the Master find fulfillment in the creation of His hands. Always demonstrate His power, His Spirit, His grace, His everything, nothing that is "mine" or "my own" but "His" and "His Own" that the people may exist only in God. Teach not with enticing words of man's wisdom but with the revelation of the Holy Ghost (1 Corinthians 2:13) so that they may exist only in God.

> *"And my speech and my preaching was not with enticing words of man's wisdom, but in demonstration of the Spirit and of power: That your faith should not stand in the wisdom of men, but in the power of God"* (1 Corinthians 2:4 – 5).

This is the essence of ministry and the central fellowship between the minister and God. He (the minister) is the priest who brings people to God. This is the mandate. If all ministers will keep to this, the Kingdom of God will be established in power and in glory and the work will be finished sooner.

These days, it is the church in the wilderness that is operating. The same laws of Moses under the leadership of Jesus is what is operating now. Jesus was that cloud. Jesus was that fire.

*"Moreover, brethren, I would not that ye should be ignorant, how that all our fathers were under the cloud, and all passed through the sea; And were all baptized unto Moses in the cloud and in the sea; And did all eat the same spiritual meat; And did all drink the same spiritual drink: for they drank of that spiritual Rock that followed them: and that Rock was Christ"* (1 Corinthians 10:1 – 4).

In the same manner, God expects you to walk in obedience to His Holy Spirit. Your focus shall be doing His will.

**THE GIFTS OF GOD SPEAK**
Do you know that you have the gift of God inside you and the gift can speak? God cannot express Himself on earth without His gifts. The Holy Spirit cannot manifest through you without His gifts. It is the gifts that introduce Him in every human being. I am talking about the gifts of power, the gifts of revelation and the gifts of expression.

The days are coming that when you speak, the gifts will jump out of you to take hold of the situation and they will stand between you and the situation. These are the days we are in now. If you are a leader and the gifts have not started speaking, it is time to start speaking. It is time to ask, "Father, where is the voice of the Holy Spirit in me? Where is the expression of the Holy Spirit in me? Wherever it is hidden within me, let it begin to speak."

You must have read in 1 Kings 18:36 where the prophet Elijah implored that if he was His servant, let fire come down from heaven and consume the offering.
*"Let them therefore give us two bullocks; and*

*let them choose one bullock for themselves, and
cut it in pieces, and lay it on wood, and put no
fire under: and I will dress the other bullock,
and lay it on wood, and put no fire under: And
call ye on the name of your gods, and I will
call on the name of the Lord: and the God that
answereth by fire, let him be God. And all the
people answered and said, It is well spoken."*
(1 Kings 18:23 – 24)

Where do you think he was speaking? He was speaking from
the vantage of the hidden mysteries that were the gifts of God
which were in him. What he wanted expressed were the gifts
of God. The sign that he is a servant of God is the coming
down of fire. The sign that you are the servant of God is gifts
expressing themselves.

**The Bible says that I am preordained from heaven to ex-
press spiritual gifts.**

> *"For we are his workmanship, created in Christ
> Jesus unto good works, which God hath before
> ordained that we should walk in them"* (Ephe-
> sians 2:10).

That is why the Bible says that the Lord has blessed us with
all spiritual blessings in heavenly places. If the gifts do not
speak, you are useless, you are hopeless. You would be most
miserable as a leader.

> *"Wherefore he saith, When he ascended up on
> high, he led captivity captive, and gave gifts
> unto men. (Now that he ascended, what is it but
> that he also descended first into the lower parts
> of the earth? He that descended is the same also*

*that ascended up far above all heavens, that he*
*might fill all things.)"* (Ephesians 4:8 – 10).

He gave gifts to men. But in Psalms, it is said that He gave gifts to all man. The phrase "to the rebellious" is used, and that book of Psalms is the root of the scripture in Ephesians 4. He gave gifts to all men. He did not choose John and leave Peter.

Ephesians 4:8 – 10 is the foundation on which you stand. It is the resurrection. It is talking about gifts. If you believe that Jesus rose, it means He rose with you and released you into His gifts. It means you are qualified for these gifts to manifest. That they are not manifesting, is your problem.

Why were the gifts given? To perfect the saints. It is these gifts that make you invisible.

*"For the perfecting of the saints, for the work*
*of the ministry, for the edifying of the body of*
*Christ: Till we all come in the unity of the faith,*
*and of the knowledge of the Son of God, unto*
*a perfect man, unto the measure of the stature*
*of the fulness of Christ"* (Ephesians 4:12 – 13).

Take away these gifts and the devil will knock you down. Every leader needs these gifts so that he can stand, so that his life can be perfected.

You criticize those whose gifts are manifesting because you are not busy with your own. It is time to look for your gifts whether you are a woman, a man or a child. Whatever you are, it is time to look for your gifts. It is time for our lives as a whole to change. The reason is for the perfection of the saints.

If you speak in tongues, you are not speaking for another person's good but for the perfection of your life.

Some of you are careless about yourselves. If you die, the church will not miss you. Let your gifts speak so that the church can benefit. When some of you pray, you say, "God give me the gifts so I can do your work." If you say that the work will prosper, you are wrong. The single truth is that you will prosper and the Body of Christ will be edified. Then the gift will continue to operate until we all come to the unity of faith and of the knowledge of the Son.

As long as you are hooked to Jesus and His manifestation, which Revelation 4 calls the seven Spirits of God, your spirit will be released. The seven Spirits of Jesus are released in order to release the life and fire of God through your spirit. It is those seven Spirits and their manifestations that speak in the different gifts. The reason why your gifts are not manifesting is that you have not seen Jesus enough. You need to see Him daily. Then your whole body will loosen and the gift of God will flow easily, not by struggle.

I do not struggle to receive revelation to be a spiritual man. All I need is to stay in His presence. If we are believers, where is the Holy Spirit since we believed? Where are the gifts? Have you received the Holy Ghost since you believed? Where are His signs manifesting through you? The way you know you have received Jesus are the signs manifesting through you. The challenge is, where are the gifts of the Holy Spirit since you became a Christian?

In Mark 16, the Bible says these signs shall follow those who believe the gospel of Jesus Christ.

*"And these signs shall follow them that believe;*

*In my name shall they cast out devils; they shall speak with new tongues; They shall take up serpents; and if they drink any deadly thing, it shall not hurt them; they shall lay hands on the sick, and they shall recover"* (Mark 16:17 – 18).

Many years ago as I was praying for a woman, I saw the gifts of the Holy Spirit in her life develop hands that were jumping out of her. One hand would jump out and take hold of one situation, uproot it and throw it into the sea. When I asked the Lord the meaning, He replied, "This is how the gifts operate." The gifts come out in power. The seven Spirits walk over all the earth. As the Lord moves you forward, He takes hold of situations and clears them. He is the wiper. Have you not read in the scripture that, "I shall go before you and make crooked places straight?" The Lord said that the gifts of the Holy Ghost are the ones that take away the crookedness out of our ways.

Is there any crookedness in your way? Forget about uprooting them if you don't want the gifts of the Holy Ghost in your life. You need not go to anybody to pray for you because it is the gifts of God in them that they will use to praying for you.

**A HIDDEN WELL**
You should begin to ask God where your gifts are hidden. Ask Him to release them to you. Jesus said to the woman at the well, *"If you knew who was speaking to you, you would ask him to give you a gift, and the gift I will give you shall be a well springing up unto everlasting life."* He did say he would give the woman living water. Jesus spoke about a gift that will become a well. It means that every individual has a well somewhere that is supposed to be serving his life. Your spiritual gift has a well, a personal well that is identified by your name. Call your name and say, "I have a secret well which was ordained from heaven that services me." If you have not identified your

well, ask the Lord Jesus to give you your well springing unto everlasting life. This means it would water you for eternity, it would bring continuity to your life. Ask the Lord to dig your well so that you can bathe in it and be swallowed by it.

When the apostles were praying, they implored God to stretch out His hand to heal in order to show that He was doing it. It was against Him that the Sanhedrin were operating. If they did not see God in action, they would think the apostles had sent themselves. So, they cried that the only way God could convince the people was by increasing the miracles. The Sanhedrin would either believe God or commit suicide – refuse to believe at all by hardening their hearts.

> *"And now, Lord, behold their threatenings: and grant unto thy servants, that with all boldness they may speak thy word, By stretching forth thine hand to heal; and that signs and wonders may be done by the name of thy holy child Jesus"* (Acts 4:29 – 30).

The apostles asked God to move by signs and wonders. It means the Lord by His hands should change situations and circumstances before the eyes of the skeptics, the scoffers and persecutors. God should affect every situation.

Isaiah thought he was a local champion in Isaiah 6. But when he came into the presence of God, he saw somebody who did a much greater, a much more spectacular miracle than he had ever seen, the One his eyes and ears had neither seen nor perceived in his lifetime.

> *"In the year that king Uzziah died I saw also the Lord sitting upon a throne, high and lifted up, and his train filled the temple. Above it stood the seraphims: each one had six wings;*

*with twain he covered his face, and with twain he covered his feet, and with twain he did fly. And one cried unto another, and said, Holy, holy, holy, is the Lord of hosts: the whole earth is full of his glory. And the posts of the door moved at the voice of him that cried, and the house was filled with smoke. Then said I, Woe is me! for I am undone; because I am a man of unclean lips, and I dwell in the midst of a people of unclean lips: for mine eyes have seen the King, the Lord of hosts"* (Isaiah 6:1 – 5).

The person simply came out and started shouting, *"Holy, holy, holy, is the Lord of hosts: the whole earth is full of his glory."* As soon as the man uttered the last word, "earth," the Bible records that the doorposts of the earth began to open. The man did not command. He did not bind or loose. He simply adored God. He was not talking to the earth. But because the earth heard the anointing from the voice of the Cherubim, the door opened.

"Ah!" Isaiah exclaimed. "I am in trouble; I am finished, my nakedness is revealed." Isaiah thought he knew God. He thought he had operated with anointing, after praying and fasting before calling heaven to answer. But the Cherubim were just praising and adoring God when the doors opened. This is the highest level of anointing; the one the Bible says, "While you are still speaking, I will answer." That is the highest peak of anointing.

When the oil, the perfect oil of leaders, begins to speak, many extra-ordinary things will happen through them. The time is coming and this is the time that, without words, while you are still pondering over the solution to a crisis situation, the miracle will take place. The anointing is coming which leaders would carry, they would set the place ablaze. There is a baptism, there is a glory that is coming, a glory that is beyond us. There is a power the Lord is preparing us to carry. I am convinced that we are being ushered into that anointing. It will be the beginning of glory in this century.

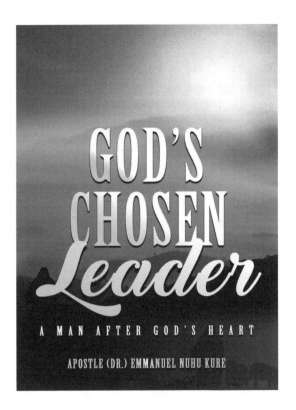

# CHAPTER 3

## Anointing By Childlike Disposition

If you want your anointing to increase, become like a suckling child. When the Bible talks about suckling babes, it not referring to a babe literally suckling a breast, far from it. God is talking about men who would speak by faith and act by faith like little children. The Kingdom of God is received as a child and you must relate to God as a child to get His Kingdom operating on your behalf. The end-time oil will take this orientation. You must pattern your orientation to be like that of a child to make the oil flow. The Bible in Psalms 8:1 – 2 corroborates this teaching about child-like orientation,

> *"O Lord our Lord, how excellent is thy name in all the earth! who hast set thy glory above the heavens. Out of the mouth of babes and sucklings hast thou ordained strength because of thine enemies, that thou mightest still the enemy and the avenger."*

This means the ones you look down on, the ones you think are incapable of doing something, would soon spring surprises. It would take a child-like nature to contend with and contain the enemies we are going to come against in the coming years. Note this: because when the time of the battle comes, this is the key that would enable you to be the victor. In the coming years, the enemies that would come against us at home, in our offices and on the street, it would take the attitude of a child, not a grown up to defeat them. It is in this disposition that God will ordain strength. Leadership is not for proud men who have something to prove, men who have an ax to grind or a score to settle. God has no need for such men in this end-time. A leader must realize that he is nothing. But in his nothingness, God is everything. The Bible says that the weakness of God is stronger than the strength of men.

> *"Because the foolishness of God is wiser than men; and the weakness of God is stronger than men. For ye see your calling, brethren, how that not many wise men after the flesh, not many mighty, not many noble, are called: But God hath chosen the foolish things of the world to*

*confound the wise; and God hath chosen the weak things of the world to confound the things which are mighty; And base things of the world, and things which are despised, hath God chosen, yea, and things which are not, to bring to nought things that are: That no flesh should glory in his presence."*

(1 Corinthians 1:25 – 29)

This is how leaders can draw strength; they should have nothing to argue about. God will raise people in your church, in your house or in your committee to speak for you, men who can prove for you. You have no point to prove except that which the Holy Spirit proves, except that which the gift in you speaks out.

What is your boasting if God does not give you a reason to boast? What is your victory if God does not give you victory? I have nothing to prove if the Lord allows my enemies to kill me. When you insist on a truth, but somebody want to fight and turn the truth to lies, stop fighting about it. If God be God, He would meet him on the way.

Remember the old and the young prophet,
> *"And when he was gone, a lion met him by the way, and slew him: and his carcase was cast in the way, and the ass stood by it, the lion also stood by the carcase. And, behold, men passed by, and saw the carcase cast in the way, and the lion standing by the carcase: and they came and told it in the city where the old prophet dwelt."*
> (1 Kings 13:24 – 25)

The young prophet disobeyed. God met him on the way in a devouring lion. Death was his judgment. May God save us.

Remember also the judgment of God over Miriam because of her rude and cutting remarks against Moses,

> *"And Miriam and Aaron spake against Moses because of the Ethiopian woman whom he had married: for he had married an Ethiopian woman. And they said, Hath the Lord indeed spoken only by Moses? hath he not spoken also by us? And the Lord heard it* (Numbers 12:1 – 2).

It is clear by all human standards that Moses had erred by marrying an Ethiopian woman instead of a Jew. But one would expect God to pronounce his disappointment and consequent judgment. Instead, Miriam and Aaron had the audacity to dress Moses down instead of entreating him. Perhaps they assumed he was their brother and as such they could speak to him that way. This kindled God's anger against Miriam.

> *"And the anger of the Lord was kindled against them; and he departed. And the cloud departed from off the tabernacle; and, behold, Miriam became leprous, white as snow: and Aaron looked upon Miriam, and, behold, she was leprous."*
> (Numbers 12:9 – 10)

Before God's judgment upon Miriam, He had spoken extensively to defend Moses.

> *"And he said, Hear now my words: If there be a prophet among you, I the Lord will make myself known unto him in a vision, and will speak unto him in a dream. My servant Moses is not so, who is faithful in all mine house. With him will I speak mouth to mouth, even apparently, and not in dark speeches; and the similitude of the*

*Lord shall he behold: wherefore then were ye*
*not afraid to speak against my servant Moses?"*
(Numbers 12:6 – 8)

When David retired to the battle camp to give his elder brother food, he met the people of Israel under the threat, torment and taunting of the giant for forty days. For forty taunting days they had cringed in fear. But when David came to King Saul, he narrated his child-like experience in the bush; how he delivered his father's sheep from the mouth of lions and bear and killed the lion. He assured the King that the Lord who enabled him to slay the lion and bear would make the giant Goliath fall into his hands since this uncircumcised Philistine had defied the armies of the living God.

*"David said moreover, The Lord that delivered*
*me out of the paw of the lion, and out of the paw*
*of the bear, he will deliver me out of the hand of*
*this Philistine. And Saul said unto David, Go,*
*and the Lord be with thee"* (1 Samuel 17:37).

Having been allowed to fight the battle and having discarded the armor (the carnal weapon) and like a child chose five stones from a brook along with his sling, he smote the most dreaded giant with a stone. This is the mystery of a child-like disposition; it is the complete surrender of the power from on high.

We have come to the period of the child-like disposition. With it we shall rule cities; we shall rule nations; we shall rule situations. These years have the anointing that will make ministries prosper. When ministries who think they have made it boast of their achievements and look down upon you, just keep quiet. It is not by boasting that doors are opened. Leave them alone; just get back to hiding and seek for Him who called you to examine your countenance and clean any mess that does not allow people to see the glory of God in your life. Go back to Him who called you, He who ordained you, and let Him answer back in the open place. When you step out one day, you will find out that you have become bigger than all of them.

When you withdraw from answering back, the day your enemies look at you, they would discover that you are far ahead of them, far beyond their reach. Do you know that it is by response that your enemies assess your strength? It is by your answer that your enemies know your strength. Do not tell your enemy that you are weak. Do not tell those who seek your downfall, otherwise you are finished. No wonder Moses could only confide in God that he stammered. He dared not tell Pharaoh that; Pharaoh would kill him. Having known his secret, Pharaoh would have taken advantage of him.

Some believers have always undressed themselves by their big mouth, by their pride. They are easily agitated. When somebody wants to hurt you, he would first step on your toes. And then you start boasting, "I am the son of this, I came from this …" You have just told him your strength: you are frightened, and by your fear his strength is increased. If he never knew your strength, he would be careful to step on your toes lest he marched on to where your strength is uppermost.

It is time for quietness in the coming years. It is not time for boasting. Let nobody predict you. Otherwise, you are done for. This is part of the secrets of surviving the years to come.

# Personal Notes

_____

_____

_____

_____

_____

_____

_____

_____

_____

_____

_____

_____

_____

_____

_____

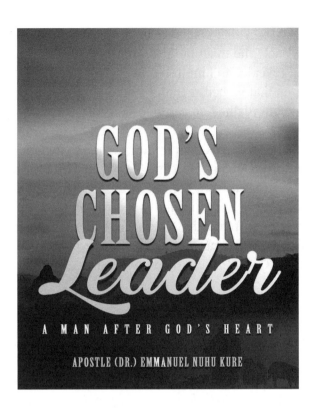

# CHAPTER
# 4

## Working According To The Fashion In Heaven

The focus of any ministry is as revealed by the Lord.

> *"Our fathers had the tabernacle of witness in the wilderness, as he had appointed, speaking unto Moses, that he should make it according to the fashion that he had seen"* (Acts 7:44).

God told Moses that whatever he did on earth when he built the tabernacle, he must build it according to the pattern that had been revealed to him in heaven. This is because it is only the fashion that he had seen that could uproot everything that God had not ordained on earth.

Each time God came down to any of the prophets in the Old and New Testaments, He came down in His chariots. The chariots God used were built according to the fashion of the throne of God in heaven. That is the reason God told Moses to be careful to build the tabernacle according to the fashion which he had seen revealed to him from heaven. Moses was led by God Himself. They walked together all through his years.

A minister's life is an open book with God. They do it together. The minister does not do it for God. They do it together.

> *"Which also our fathers that came after brought in with Jesus into the possession of the Gentiles, whom God drave out before the face of our fathers, unto the days of David"* (Acts 7:45).

Note that Jesus Himself was always careful to walk according to the fashion of His Father in heaven.

> *"Then answered Jesus and said unto them, Verily, verily, I say unto you, The Son can do nothing of himself, but what he seeth the Father do: for what things soever he doeth, these also doeth the Son likewise"* (John 5:19).

The ministry's focus and vision is to walk according to the pattern laid down in scripture. At the initial call to this ministry, God told me "My son, do not go for the trivial. Do not go for the mundane, nor for the one that shows off. You shall wait upon me and that which you see me unfold, it is only that you will also do. You shall be a chronicle and an answer of what you see."

A chronicler is he who speaks only that which he sees whether that which he speaks is pleasant to the hearer or not. Paul said he that runs the race must run according to the rules or he has no reward for his efforts.

Only he who walks according to the fashion in heaven will succeed. He who walks in this fashion will act and move as the Spirit of God directs and instructs. Everyman's oil has a message and a direction. It is the oil that carries the individual and not the individual carrying the oil. Great men of God in scripture acted by this fashion because they had the right oils. It gave the right direction. Philip, Paul, Peter, name them, acted and walked in this fashion and did great exploits for the Lord.

When you allow the Spirit of God, the oil in your life to lead you, you will enter places where others have failed and **you will succeed.**

There are two greatest things in the heart of the Lord. One is the harvest of as many souls as can be saved from the world before it is folded up and a new heaven and a new earth begins. This cry and program started since Adam fell in the Garden of Eden. This is the Spirit of Prophecy that Jesus personifies. That is what the very life, ministry and existence of Jesus, both on the earth and in heaven, represents.

Every minister's life revolves, or must revolve around reaping, or keeping (sustaining, shepherding and glorifying) the harvest. Any ministry outside this is NOT of God. There is no ministry for making money. Those who personify greed in ministry are anti-Christ. Stay away from them, lest they adulterate your oils.

In Matthew 21:33, you will notice that in God's plan for the earth, there is only provision for the harvest – winepress – and the tower. It is only by the tower that the winepress can be taken care of. The two are irrevocably fused together. Elisha lived on a tower and ruled kings, kingdoms and peoples of different nations from there. You must learn to live in a tower as a watchman, a prayer warrior who dwells and breathes only from the presence of the Lord to accomplish God's will and to walk in His direction and have eternal accomplishments. Your tower (prayer life) must be built for our harvest to be through. This is the approach to accomplishing God's will that the Lord has given, which the ministry I head personifies. Let us go to the divine harvest by power built and gotten from our watchtowers.

It is the watchtower that links us to the Melchizedek (Jesus) priesthood in heaven and their flow. Jesus lived and breathed prayer. Day and night, he lived in solitude with God either in the mountains in the night, or at every given quiet opportunity. It is time to be like Him for the harvest to be accomplished.

**THE JERUSALEM COUNCIL**
We are coming back to the time when there shall be much confusion (it may not be in the organized form). But God is going to raise a kind of mini-Jerusalem council all over the world and there would be leaders over them. And these leaders shall become signet leaders that would give wise counsel to calm the storm.

Every ministry is a manifestation of that kind of body, a body anointed to give signals. It shall give signals to churches, apostles, bishops and tell them how to go. God is creating true symbols. I know that a day is coming that the praying groups in Nigeria will join hands together and shake this nation. They will not gather to debate national issues; it is not their business. They will link up the Jerusalem council, they will become signs unto the nation. Paul and Peter would quarrel, yet they never broke up the council. But today, when we quarrel, we break up the council. The senior pastor dares not correct his junior, the junior pastor would break up and start on his own. All they are looking for is bread and butter anointing.

Mordecai was not a church leader in Israel. Nobody knew Mordecai. He was a servant at the gate of the king who dictated the lives of Israel. Mordecai established the Esther. Mordecai was a watchman from where he was; but he decided the pace, the emotions, the behavior of the people. He was a signet. A signet is a ring, a seal. It is with the signet of a king that a thing is established. If the king turns it against you, you are as good as dead. But if the king turns it for you, you will prosper. If he puts his signet on a thing, it is established forever. The signet is the sign of the emotion of the king.

God told Zerubbabel, *"I will make you the sign of my emotion."* You will notice that when Jesus Christ was born, the Bible says "he shall be an ensign" that is the sign of God's emotion. A leader is the sign of God's emotion. He is like a sign; people will inquire what he knows what he says over an issue. That is why mostly at the beginning of the year or at critical situations, you hear people asking what Rev. Adeboye says, what Bishop Oyedepo says, what Pastor Kure says, what the prophesy is for the new year. Why? This is because these people are supposed to be signs because leaders are signs and pace setters.

You must turn your life to become the one that sets the pace. I am not just talking about giving leadership. I am talking about your personal life. If you are a woman, a man, a wife or a husband, turn your life to set the pace. Your house must set the pace for others to copy. It will not only give you strength, it will give the church outside strength. We are pacesetters. The day the angels come asking for the houses they can visit, your house will be named. When angels come, they go into the houses of the pacesetters, not the houses of the chief leaders; but they go into the houses of those who are the signets and that includes you.

I believe angels are coming, if they have not started coming. You know why I believe that? There is no dispensation where God came down from heaven without angels going before Him to herald His coming. Our generation will not stop it. When God was to lead Israel to Canaan land, an angel was sent in His name who said to Moses, "Give me your hand for we are going to Canaan land." It means right now thousands of angels you cannot see are being released and prepared and armed to lead you and your families to the place of glory and unto the coming king, to prepare and adorn the bride for the groom. Jesus is coming for a glorious church prepared by angels; and their glorious church is you, the signet.

Do you know that the Jerusalem council was the representation of the real church, the voice and the mind of God? The Jerusalem council was the signet God used in early days to check the church. There is always a problem when you personalize the church because it is your principle that will rule.

We are going back to the apostolic setting, administrativewise, where the church was not led by bishops but by the signet. And the signet is Jesus Christ, the Holy Spirit and there were men representing the signet. I am taking my turn. I am looking forward to the day that I will sit like Father Abraham and men shall travel from afar to inquire for the right pattern.

The reason why the church could not be broken was because there was only one voice they heard. Jesus, Paul, Silas and Barnabas could quarrel, but they remained together because there was only one voice – Jesus. Did you ever hear any church or branches break into two? Go and search your Bible. There were bishops over the churches. Paul was not a bishop, but he was a leader over the bishops. Paul was a leader over the bishops because he bore a signet. Zerubbabel was made a signet, he was a sign of the emotions of God.

# Personal Notes

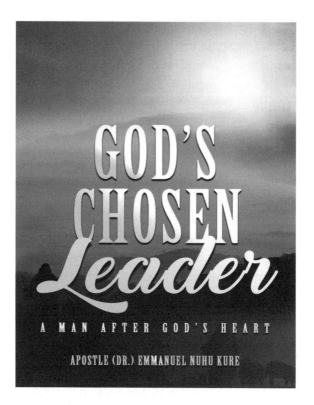

# CHAPTER 5

## Why The Devil Attacks The Vision

Every vision faces a threat from the pit of hell because the devil does not want it to survive. Everyone involved in carrying out a vision will face all kinds of hardships because the devil is out to destroy the vision. The devil aims at attacking the vision first. He fights the vision very hard, and it is with pain and travail that the Vision is born and sustained.

The vision must not die whatever the situation or circumstance because in the day when the vision dies, the world will say righteousness is dead and unrighteousness is glorified. One must strive to keep the vision alive unto blood. There is no vision without travail. The devil attacks the vision you are carrying out because it represents God's reign on earth. He is attacking the vision of God in you which he tried to attack through Jesus but failed because God threw him out. He feels that by so doing he will stop that altar of witness from going on. We are the continuation of God's work on earth and the devil is out to stop us. When the devil attacks your business, source of wealth, and fails and your business is established well on the ground, it becomes a secret wealth that will support and sustain the work of God.

However, it is possible for one to carry on the vision but not to enjoy the fruit of his labor. Moses was such a man who fought the lions and faced all kinds of hazards. He only had a glimpse of the Promised Land, but he could not get into it. Who stopped him? The dragon. The dragon will usually strike when carelessness comes in. When the individual begins to lose his vision and focus, then the devil strikes.

When God makes was for His program, He always makes way for the messenger, protecting the oracle and keeping the oracle alive to carry on with God's program. The only demand that God makes of us is righteousness and faithfulness in the execution of our duties. At Gethsemane, just when Jesus was looking to the cross, He was about to step to the last point where He would take the keys of hell and finish the last job, at that point, His heart almost failed Him. But He resisted by travail even unto blood. That's why He had victory. That is also what we have to face as a ministry.

As a matter of fact, this ministry has faced a lot of struggles right from the beginning both in the physical and spiritual. The peak of the struggles surfaced in 1997 when everything the ministry had and stood for was threatened. The devil thought he could attack the vision through the vision coordinator. I was threatened by death on several occasions in 1997 not only by sickness but by an assassination attempt. There were crises among staff in 1997 more than has ever been since the beginning of the ministry. About five of the staff had to go; some by dismissal and some by withdrawal of service.

The building project almost came to a standstill when at a point, the flow of money just ceased. But through tears, groaning and persistence, conscious of the vision, the Lord kept us and brought a resurrection by the end of the year in each of these areas that the ministry was threatened. Staff that left the ministry were replaced twice in number by high quality staff. And the building picked up by miraculous provisions. To crown it all, the Lord gave me reassurance of life.

The devil is not interested in you; he is interested in what you represent and what you will accomplish for God. He is not interested in your house or car but is interested in what you represent that is God. It is because the purpose of God in your life cannot be carried out except by God Himself. When Satan resists it, he has stopped God.

Who told you that you are suffering? You are not. I want you to change the language of battle. Any time you find yourself suffering, attack the devil by addressing your warfare to the vision the Lord called you to accomplish. For instance, if you are a pastor and have a ministry and suddenly you find out that nothing is working out again. Or you are a medical doctor and you have a hospital and suddenly the hospital starts going down; patients are dying, things are going wrong. Do not say the devil is attacking you. He is not, he is attacking the vision.

So, when you talk to the hospital, talk to it as a vision and say, "This vision cannot be destroyed. It is the oil of the Lord. It is written, touch not my anointed. Do my prophets no harm." Go ahead and touch the walls of your hospital or ministry and say, "Oh hospital, oh ministry, the fire of the Lord that created you burn the cankerworms that are eating you. I release that fire to begin to burn now. I say, cankerworm, begin to die in this place in Jesus' name."

It is the vision that is being attacked, not man. They are not interested in you. They are interested in the church. They are interested in the work you can accomplish for the Lord. They are interested in your salvation. The Bible says fight the good fight of faith because the battle is the battle of faith. When the devil attacks, it is your faith that he is attacking, not you. You may ask, what is the difference between me and my faith?

The difference is that one takes you to heaven; the other one if left alone will die. The difference is that your faith is equal to God. When the devil came down, did he say he hated Adam? He had no business with Adam. But he had to cut off the sweet flow between God and Adam. That is what the devil attacked. That call of God that is not prospering is a covenant call. Speak to it. Speak to the purpose for which it was established. And when you address that purpose, the anointing will begin to heal from the root. It will hear the voice of the oil of that purpose. When the oil of God begins to move, everything that stands in the way; the oil will trample it because the oil is God.

The shame of this hour is that many have lost the vision. The shepherds are there to feed themselves.

> *"Son of man, prophesy against the shepherds of Israel, prophesy, and say unto them, Thus saith the Lord God unto the shepherds; Woe be to*

*the shepherds of Israel that do feed themselves!*
*should not the shepherds feed the flocks?"*

(Ezekiel 34:2)

That is the shame of this hour. A great number of pastors are there to feed themselves. They are going to die before their time because they are exploiting those who are diseased. Be careful what you are doing. Gehazi got leprous and I am afraid that many ministers are following his habits.

The greatest temptation you get in ministry is greed, to go behind like Gehazi and collect what their masters have rejected. They will collect and the leprosy of those men shall follow them. The man has a suffering. He is sowing a seed for God to lift his suffering. But you are behind to collect the seed.

When you do so, you collect his sufferings as well because the anointing of that seed has to do with suffering. So, why don't you allow the seed to go to the altar it belongs to that the healing of that suffering will come. It is not wrong that the man is sowing for his suffering. But it is wrong to divert the seed.

From now on, there shall be an Elisha priesthood, an Elisha anointing, not Gehazi's. He was the one who held the bag for Elijah and took over for him. Gehazi came, held the bag, but got leprosy instead. Do you not know that the day you take advantage of one that is in trouble, when you know within you that the unction of the Spirit is not there to heal that situation, you are transferring the infirmity of that situation to yourself?

I asked God why he does not disgrace his ministers openly? He said, "Because I punish them in their houses." I asked how, and he said, "I punish them through their children, through their wives, in their hearts and in their bodies. They will not tell the world the truth. The reason why I do not disgrace them openly is that if I do, I disgrace myself." That made me to be patient with the false and unfaithful ministers. Since God is not disgracing them, it is not my anointing to go about disgracing them. If the master wants, let him make them like Gehazi.

Another way the devil attacks the vision of God is insincerity in the church which is the greatest problem in the church today. Elders cannot trust their pastors, and pastors cannot trust their elders either. The king is coming There is going to be a church that will walk in the wilderness. Will you choose to be part of the wilderness anointing or will you choose to be part of the darkness or be part of the glory of the church? There are going to be two kinds of people: the harlot and the glorious church. The harlot church will speak for the darkness that is coming. The glorious church will speak against the darkness.

Where will you belong? People of God, the Spirit that rules us is called the Spirit of truth. The greatest power in your anointing is "truth." It is that anointing that makes the dead rise. What makes your healing partial is the lack of truth in the ingredients of your oil. I want to say this, if you do not want to die before your time, allow God's transparency to rule in your life. If you do not want to be like Gehazi, do the kingdom work the way it should be done. Otherwise, you may be leprous, Your craftiness may save you today, it will not keep you forever. Even when you are seeing increase, if your integrity is under question, it is time to go back and catch the oil to protect you. Do not take your success for granted. Otherwise, your success will vanish before your eyes.

Whether you like it or not, we are going back to the apostolic age. And the apostolic age is not going to be made up of singular local champions. It is going to be made up of people of power. God wants to lift you up as an individual. This is time to warn women to stop using their husbands as an excuse not to work for God. The Bible says that you are the secret place of the dwelling of your husband. That means that you are a shield to your husband.

That is why when your husband has a sickness or business that cannot be healed, you are to blame yourself. This is because there is an oil element in a woman that heals. That is why she was brought out from the rib. So, do not rejoice that you are original when you are a balm and a healing to the one you came to complete. If a woman loves God like Deborah and Anna the prophets, she will have good fellowship with him. In the day of the travail of her husband and children, if she carries the travail to God and talks to him as a sign, and a wailing woman, God will hear and answer instantly.

When Israel was in trouble, Isaiah said, "Call the wailing women and we shall cry with them and our healing shall come." Poor Moses, the man would have died, a whole man of God. It was the woman who was always in the background, the wife, that saved him. There is that situation that will come upon you, your husband or your house, that nobody would be able to solve except you. There will always be that situation because of the oil on you. It takes your cry to being down the oil. In this end time, three groups of people hold the key. They are the elders, the wailing women and the virgin daughters of men. That is those who have kept their garments pure.

## AN OBSESSION OF VISION
Except the vision in your life becomes an obsession, it cannot succeed. It must drive you, push you, disturb you and make you restless. Without this panicle in your vision, you cannot carry the fire power that accomplishes anything. The Bible calls this kind of obsession ZEAL. It possesses you like a spirit, takes you captive, eats you up and makes you helpless and

a slave to its wish. The disciples had this testimony of Jesus,

*"And his disciples remembered that it was written, The zeal of thine house hath eaten me up"* (John 2:17).

This is the only power that could make Jesus face the cross. It is the only thing that makes you stand the storm and pressures of ministry. It is the only burning that can make you stand all odds.

Every vision that becomes an obsession cannot fail. It will always create doors by the power of conviction behind it for it to succeed. Heaven must eat up your soul with its will for your life. Search your vision. If it is not making you restless yet, it means it is not from God or your hour has not come.

Many run into ministry without enough obsession and driving force, and soon enough they run out of focus. Heaven must baptize you with a spirit of burning before you step out; otherwise, don't. It takes a fire to be in ministry and not just a mere calling.

The way you can judge whether God said you are an Apostle is you seeing the oil of the Apostle manifesting, not the title.

Anybody that the Lord calls, he ordains. Manifest it and then we shall know you have that calling. That is why I don't like big titles. That is why if a minister comes to me and talks to me about his church, I tell him to prove his calling. When you prove your calling, then I know you are that minister. Otherwise, your ministry is for your belly. I know those ministers who just go into ministry to make money. They are there just to gather people, then begin to make it. They don't have a vision. Their vision is for their stomach. But a minister that has anointing, the anointing makes him restless toward the pattern of his calling. So, he restlessly goes about fulfilling it.

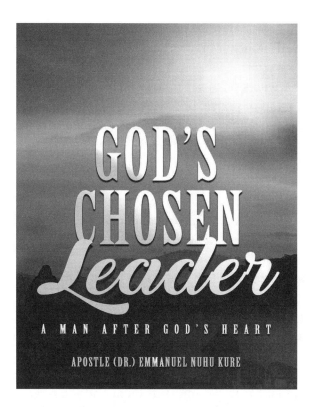

# CHAPTER
# 6

# The Governance In Heaven

The Lord is lifting men up as they humble themselves because humility means lifting up. If you see yourself as a priest, first you will minister as a priest. But when you see yourself as a special entity, you are lost because eventually, you will find out that you do not edify your congregation but entertain them A minister should speak as a priest, minister as a priest and worship God not men. He should forget the men around and carry the people into the presence of God and he will find out that he will minister grace like he has never done before.

The Lord wants us to separate ourselves unto Him as vessels of honor and of praise; and we are about to become one with heaven. As heaven is, so are we, so shall we become. Everything about us will bear fruit. When we speak, it will bear fruit. When we walk or smile, it shall bear fruit.

> *"And he shewed me a pure river of water of life, clear as crystal, proceeding out of the throne of God and of the Lamb"* (Revelations 22:1).

The pipe through which that water flows is the individual. As we allow this water to flow through us, we will be clear as crystal and everything about our lives will be clear. Again, in the midst of the streets (in heaven) on either side of the river was the tree of life. Adam was planted inside of them. There was a tree of life and a tree of the knowledge of good and evil. He was planted in the midst of them and the river had to go through him. On both sides was a tree of life which bore all manner of fruits and yielded its fruits every month and the leaves of the tree were for the healing of the nations.

The mystery behind the tree bearing fruit was the river. Adam was made to take care of the inhabitants. It was his business to water all the trees including the tree of life and the tree of the knowledge of good and evil. Every morning, he had to take care of them. He had a way of getting them watered. He was the life of God who took care of the garden. He gave animals their names.

The beauty of it (the garden) was not the trees but the lamb. This river reminds us of Zerubabel in Zechariah chapter 4 where the oil flowed from heaven, from the golden pipes.

And that oil went through Zerubabel as a channel. That meant anything Zerubabel touched from that time became fruitful: his voice became fruitful. His smile brought healing, things changed.

The Lord sits inside a wheel where there were coals of fire and He walks in the wheel. Elijah got carried by the chariots of fire, and in Revelations 4:1 – 5, John said, the anointing that will bring back Jesus is the ANOINTING OF FIRE.

> *"After this I looked, and, behold, a door was opened in heaven: and the first voice which I heard was as it were of a trumpet talking with me; which said, Come up hither, and I will shew thee things which must be hereafter. And immediately I was in the spirit: and, behold, a throne was set in heaven, and one sat on the throne. And he that sat was to look upon like a jasper and a sardine stone: and there was a rainbow round about the throne, in sight like unto an emerald. And round about the throne were four and twenty seats: and upon the seats I saw four and twenty elders sitting, clothed in white raiment; and they had on their heads crowns of gold. And out of the throne proceeded lightnings and thunderings and voices: and there were seven lamps of fire burning before the throne, which are the seven Spirits of God."*
> (Revelation 4:1 – 5)

On the throne round about, were not only the twenty-four elders, but seven lamps of fire. And the Bible said that they are not just fire – they are spirits. In that one verse is the summary of the government of heaven sitting in governance. That is the judgment seat sitting in its beauty. This is the council of

God that makes decisions over the earth. John said, "He that cometh after me shall baptize you with the Holy Ghost and with fire." Part of the governance in heaven is carried out by fire and the life in that fire is called the seven spirits of God.

This government is summarized in Revelation chapter four and that is where the real thing is happening. The elders have the oil and the mystery in their lips to turn around the destiny of a nation. The right elders in the church are those that have not corrupted their garments or their tongue; those who are not lost yet they are the only hope along with the virgin daughters of Zion, not just women but everyone that has kept his garment unspoiled, like in the days of Sennacherib, and saved Israel. The wailing women knew the oil that they carried in their bodies.

The government in heaven governs the earth. It makes decisions and that is where the altar of sacrifice is. Our petitions are carried to and poured on that altar. The angels stay lower than that government. Those sitting around are sitting in their high-thrones, and every time, thrones were surrounded by the rainbow – the twenty-four elders and seven lamps. The language of the seven lamps is fire meaning that the earth shall be governed by fire in these last days. That is why the man said he was taken into the spirit to show him what will happen hereafter (Revelation 4:1 – 5).

These twenty-four elders had crowns of gold on their heads which show that they are rulers and out of the thrones proceeded lightening. The character of the thrones is to release lightening and thundering. Remember that the first day the Holy Ghost came down, the Bible says the place shook when He came down. He didn't look like a dove but like tongues of fire (Acts 2:2 – 4). This was the beginning of the apostolic age which is with this present-day church. It shall also be the end of the church.

That means it is by fire that the church will be manifested. It is our generation that will experience what Paul said, that eyes have not seen or ears heard the things the Lord prepared for them that love Him. The anointing that is carried by fire is going to move through our bones so that anything we do will have a thundering effect.

## ROLE AWAY THE STONE

Open up and fellowship with God. Once you make contact with God, your miracle will begin. The Bible says the hour cometh when the true worshipers will worship God in spirit and in truth. It is your ability to make contact with Him that brings you the revelation you have always wanted from Him. God wants to establish a true fellowship between you and Him.

Everything you do from now on must be to honor the One Who died for you. The people of Israel were complaining that they had cried all day long, but no answer was forthcoming from God. They asked, where are the days when they manifested His power, and the nations shook before them? What took away the water of life that affected their lives? Why had their rivers gone dry?

In these days, many people are experiencing dryness. The Lord says you must roll the stone that has been rolled upon your house and upon your doors. Until you push the stone out of the gates of your own hearts – your own life, your oil will not speak again. Many of you will begin to roll off stones.

Our fellowship is with the Father and not with man. Hence the mystery of our existence is the mystery of God. Let us have a fellowship with the Spirit, a service with God. Let us begin to have a true fellowship where God comes and takes over. Let us have a service where people do not struggle to flow in the spirit. They struggle to flow in the anointing, but the miracles do not open up because the fellowship is not in spirit and truth.

Many Christians need to dig out the thing they used to do to be able to find out the oils of God: habits that are contrary to God. Situations that attract the devil and bring about blockage against the workings and the liberty of the Holy Spirit in our existence must be done away with. They must be destroyed in order to release your oils. The fellowship is to break open the hidden oils. The hidden oils must be loosened.

Every believer is expected to perform miracles. Healing is not necessarily a gift of the Spirit when it come to the general manifestation of the power and finger of God in the individual life. It is a fellowship of the Spirit, not a gift. The Bible says, "These things shall follow them that believe. In my name they shall cast out demons." It is not a gift of the Spirit. It follows those believers who fellowship.

Do you know that around your environment, your life is supposed to be a mystery? People fear herbalists and strong, medicine men. They are supposed to fear you much more. In the day when Moses arose, God made him a God over a god, and that god was Pharaoh. The Bible says the power behind Pharaoh was the dragon in the River Nile, the spirit of leviathan, the most powerful demon in the kingdom of darkness. So, when leviathan said, "I am god," he was speaking by the power of the stamp of the authority of Satan. And God said, "Behold, I make you a God over leviathan. Leviathan shall serve you. The same way you tremble before God, leviathan should tremble at your sight."

The Bible says the mountain saw and fled. That is the place of glory that God is eventually bringing you to. You are supposed to eventually become a mystery. Every Christian that does not become a mystery eventually, has not begun to flow in this race properly. He is a periphery Christian, neither cold nor hot. You are supposed to be the representative of God on earth. At your sight, the power should speak.

So what has robbed you of your miracles? The Lord says we must look inward. Otherwise, the release of the oil that brings earthquakes will not be released unto us. There is an oil that makes the earth divide into two at your sight. There is an oil that makes the mountains begin to fear, run and melt. There is an oil that make hell convene meetings night and day because they are fighting your revelation. And in these last days, you are about to enter those sacred oils that, when you are clothed by them, the kingdom of this world will become the Kingdom of our God.

Forget about the problems that are confronting you. Drink of the fountain first and the problems will disappear. When you bow before God in worship, the sickness will disappear by itself. Let your soul hear His voice first because your soul is the channel, the doorway by which hands reach your sickness. If your soul cannot hear His voice, your sickness cannot hear His voice either. It is only when your soul hears His voice that your sickness melts away. When Jesus appeared, infirmities disappeared. Your heart is the entry point of God's mercy for you when you appeal for your infirmities. When you catch a revelation of Him, your situation will catch a revelation of Him too. Therefore, your situation can be controlled by Him.

## LOOK AT THE SPIRIT OF PROPHECY
> *"And after that he gave unto them judges about the space of four hundred and fifty years, until Samuel the prophet. And afterward they desired a king: and God gave unto them Saul the son*

*of Cis, a man of the tribe of Benjamin, by the space of forty years. And when he had removed him, he raised up unto them David to be their king; to whom also he gave testimony, and said, I have found David the son of Jesse, a man after mine own heart, which shall fulfil all my will. Of this man's seed hath God according to his promise raised unto Israel a Saviour, Jesus: When John had first preached before his coming the baptism of repentance to all the people of Israel. And as John fulfilled his course, he said, Whom think ye that I am? I am not he. But, behold, there cometh one after me, whose shoes of his feet I am not worthy to loose. Men and brethren, children of the stock of Abraham, and whosoever among you feareth God, to you is the word of this salvation sent."*
(Acts 13:20 – 26)

In this year you must look at the clouds. You must not look at the environment. You must look at the spirit of prophecy. The spirit of prophecy says, "The hour is come." No matter what the situation says, the spirit of prophecy says, "The hour is come." What hour is come? This is the hour of your glorification in the Lord Jesus Christ.

The grain of wheat must die. If it refuses to die, God will not come alive in it. Who is that grain of wheat? The believer is the grain because the Bible says the seed of the woman shall bruise the seed of the serpent. The seed that must bruise must die first to be able to bruise. The corn is a seed. If you die, Jesus will resurrect you and the word of God will come alive in you. As. Long as you allow the world to rule your soul, you will abide alone.

If any man serves the Lord, him would God honor. If you serve the Lord, where is your honor? What has gone wrong?

If any man serves me, he must follow me. Follow Him all the way without reservation. The key to your honor is **following Him**.

Where does God dwell? As long as we are in the earth and have not gone to meet with the father, the father dwells in the midst of fire, the seven Spirits of God. He dwells in the midst of the seven candlesticks. He dwells in the midst of the twenty-four elders. He dwells in the midst of Fire, according to Revelation 4. The visions of God in heaven. Whose fire? His own fire: the clothing of God is His own fire.

The mystery of the Godhead in these last days is the mystery of fire. It will take fire for Nigeria to change. What does the Bible mean by "You must hate your life." It means you must abandon your life to the safe keeping of the word so that by the foolishness of the word, the wisdom of the wise might be broken for you. It is when you lose your life to the word of God – that is when you are following Him. And He says, "Where I am, there shall my servant be also." Where is Jesus Christ? In the midst of the chariots of fire.

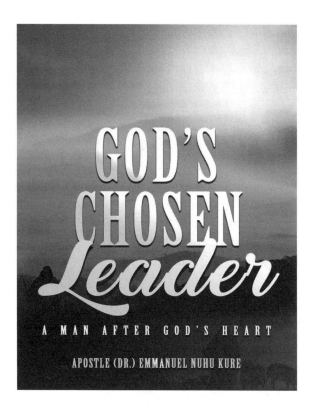

# CHAPTER
# 7

## Transfer Of Anointing

Saints with anointing; great men with double anointing die of sickness. So do not condemn your pastors when they fall sick. Why did God allow sickness to kill Elisha?

> *"Now Elisha was fallen sick of his sickness whereof he died. And Joash the king of Israel came down unto him, and wept over his face,*

*and said, O my father, my father, the chariot of Israel, and the horsemen thereof. And Elisha said unto him, Take bow and arrows. And he took unto him bow and arrows. And he said to the king of Israel, Put thine hand upon the bow. And he put his hand upon it: and Elisha put his hands upon the king's hands. And he said, Open the window eastward. And he opened it. Then Elisha said, Shoot. And he shot. And he said, The arrow of the Lord's deliverance, and the arrow of deliverance from Syria: for thou shalt smite the Syrians in Aphek, till thou have consumed them"* (2 Kings 13:14 – 17).

Elisha who made heaven to stand still; he that made kings tremble, that calleth lions for children without blinking his eyes. Elisha that made dead bodies come alive, also died of sickness. The Bible did not say he went through terrible pain. But it was sickness that killed him. Alas, Elisha who made life to bloom died of sickness.

At the end of Elisha's life, he was a man of sorrow. A man of sorrow, not because of lack or sickness, but because there was no one to transfer the anointing to. It is the most painful thing in the life of any prophet or minister when there is nobody to continue the lineage, no body to hand over. There was no son of the prophet that was qualified. Maybe that is what brought Elisha the sickness. That is why even in his death, his bones were still protesting; they made the dead to rise to show that there was no one who took the anointing.

The anointing of Elijah was never spoken after he had left because it was transferred into another man Elisha. Just as in traditional practices where witchcraft is transferred, anointing can be transferred. The sickness that killed Elisha was a sickness of the heart. There are other things I can use to prove that it was a sickness of the heart. He knew he was going, so he did not fight it; he did not struggle to put it off. He had fought a good fight. It was time to go home for the generation is an unwilling generation.

The oil will not stop with my generation. It will not stop with my pastor. It will not stop with my father; the oil must continue with me. It must not stop with the elders I am seeing. When they go, I must continue the work.

Where are the mantle bearer that will take over from here? Where are the baton receivers? Where are they? Or is the generation lost? Where are the prophets? A generation of priests is dying. Where is the generation that will take over? If pastor Kure goes home to be with the Lord tomorrow or if God gives him into the hands of a government that does not know his word, who will continue with the vision? If there comes a government that does not recognize a man of God and cuts off his head, where are the men that will take over? The day the Lord takes Pastor Adeboye into glory, will the crowd at his night vigils still be there?

You may say, "God forbid, may it never happen." But it is the reality of life. There is a day that every man must rest. In the day of his rest, where is the anointing that takes over? Or will Nigeria remain without prophets? What happens to Deeper Life when Pastor Williams Kumuyi turns his back into glory and rests in the bosom of his God? What happens to Living Faith when Bishop David Oyedepo turns his back into the earth and walks into the realm of glory? Or what is the future of the Church of God International now that Papa Idahosa is gone?

The greatest fear of any man of anointing is discontinuity. I fear about that for my own life. When I look at souls all over this nation who have breathed the direction of God and seem to be catching it, but the perfection has not come, I wonder what happens to them if anything happens to me.

I fear there are many people today whose only reason for being in these fore-mentioned churches is miracle. They are not carrying the oil. Out of 100%, 95% of those who gather in their hundreds of thousands are for miracles, cover, protection, security. Most of them do not have fellowship with the father. You must sit there and have fellowship with God so that the oil can rest upon you, so that your ministers can have rest. This will give us the assurance that in the day when we turn our back to this earth and go to the heavens, you will continue the race.

It is time to sober down and begin to think. Open up your gates to heaven, there has to be continuity. What happens to the Church of God now? Will they begin to fight and hang themselves? Everybody will claim an empire and say, "To your tents, Oh Israel!" The Jeroboam spirit will take over and the kingdom will be divided.

Was that the purpose of God in releasing the oil? It is enough to make a man sick. Some of you do not know that might be part of the worries of most general overseers now. "Oh God, where be the men of oil?" As the men of oil, we are disappointed when men we think will take over the baton in the ministries begin to run away. The future of the Church is in the oil – the anointing. But except there be men that will carry it correctly, the oil will be wasted; it will not speak again.

The Bible did not record that Elisha was afflicted by Satan. It was the sickness of the heart. If it were an affliction of Satan, he would not have died of it. It was a sickness of the heart.

Why should Elisha die of heart disease? It was because it was self-imposed. He refused to come out of it.

I also had my own share of sickness in 1997, but I came out of it. The anointing cannot be negotiated. The day you negotiate your anointing, you are finished. Be clear in your vision and follow it. People may not understand you, but you must follow the vision to the letter. As a minister, you must have nothing about self to build; you have no kingdom of your own. You have only one kingdom you are called to build – the Kingdom of Him that liveth forever. You must build it in all sincerity of purpose.

Then something happened. Joash the king of Israel came down and wept over Elisha's face. When he wept of his face, the spirit of prophesy came upon him. He wept over the prophet because he saw that the prophet was about to go home. And he wept, "Papa, if you leave us alone, we shall not survive." Many of you have read the scripture without knowing the meaning.

> *"Now Elisha was fallen sick of his sickness*
> *whereof he died. And Joash the king of Israel*
> *came down unto him, and wept over his face,*
> *and said, O my father, my father, the chariot of*
> *Israel, and the horsemen thereof."*
> (2 Kings 13:14)

Elisha told him to quickly take his bow and arrows. He told the king not to miss this opportunity before he went home. But instead of shooting five times, the king shot the ground three times.

> *"And Elisha said unto him, Take bow and ar-*
> *rows. And he took unto him bow and arrows.*

*And he said to the king of Israel, Put thine hand upon the bow. And he put his hand upon it: and Elisha put his hands upon the king's hands. And he said, Open the window eastward. And he opened it. Then Elisha said, Shoot. And he shot. And he said, The arrow of the Lord's deliverance, and the arrow of deliverance from Syria: for thou shalt smite the Syrians in Aphek, till thou have consumed them. And he said, Take the arrows. And he took them. And he said unto the king of Israel, Smite upon the ground. And he smote thrice, and stayed. And the man of God was wroth with him, and said, Thou shouldest have smitten five or six times; then hadst thou smitten Syria till thou hadst consumed it: whereas now thou shalt smite Syria but thrice. And Elisha died, and they buried him. And the bands of the Moabites invaded the land at the coming in of the year"* (2 Kings 13:15 – 20).

In the day when Elisha was to transfer anointing to a king that never deserved it, even that king missed his opportunity. The king saw the right revelations but missed the transference of that revelation. Some of you have the right revelation of God but the anointing cannot be transferred unto you because there is a slight selfishness that seems to hang on the doorway which holds back the final rest of God in your life. You must discover that seed and destroy it. Ask God to find your nakedness and take away the thorn that keeps God away from you.

There is a cry for the men who will carry the oil which will change our generation, the oil that will keep the fire burning. For a minute, Elisha became well and told Joash to take the bow and the arrow even though he did not deserve the gift. Do you know sometime God leaves the righteous men and begins to seek the unrighteous to carry the oil? May God never pass you by to pick somebody from the gutter.

If you will live by the perfect holy oil, the day will come when you will be alone in your pursuit of righteousness. At the cross, all the beloved disciples disappeared. He hung there alone. There was no one to keep him company. In the day of the suffering of Isaiah, everyone fled and left him alone to his problems. He had to complain to the Lord, "Lord, everyone has forsaken me!" He stood there in ashes and cried saying, "Where art thou? It is for your sake that I suffer this desolation."

The seed must die. It has to fall and die. Then it can live in glory. You must keep the righteousness of your heart. Then the Lord will keep you alive in the day of your troubles and His fires will burn your troubles all around you.

**COMMIT TO FAITHFUL MEN**
A minister with apostolic callings and grace must always find men that will be with him, men that will impart and transfer the grace of God into them and teach them thoroughly.

> *"And the things that thou hast heard of me among many witnesses, the same commit thou to faithful men, who shall be able to teach others also"* (2 Timothy 2:2).

They must be men the minister must wait upon God (look up to God) with to enable them to receive the same measure of his anointing so that "the works that I do shall ye do also and greater works than this shall ye do."

They shall be men who will abide with him and be used of the Holy Spirit to spread the Kingdom together with him, men who understand the difference between calling and ambition. In calling, you patiently follow it to the end, not being swayed by words of distraction. But in ambition, you will take advantage of every situation to exalt yourself, not waiting for the Holy Spirit. All you care about is your own personal success.

## LEST SOMEONE TAKE YOUR PLACE

You must learn to gain God's confidence. Elisha saw an opportunity and he cried out, "Come Joash. Take your bow and arrows." And then he made him do something else. Did you notice that the words that Joash used were the words that opened the gates of the oils that dropped upon Elisha in the day when Elijah was going?

> *"And Elisha saw it, and he cried, My father, my father, the chariot of Israel, and the horsemen thereof. And he saw him no more: and he took hold of his own clothes, and rent them in two pieces. He took up also the mantle of Elijah that fell from him, and went back, and stood by the bank of Jordan"* (2 Kings 2:12 – 13).

They were the exact words Elisha used when Elijah was taken away to heaven. Joash the king was not there. So where did he get that key from? When he fell on the prophet and started weeping, the revelation of the prophet fell upon him. That was the beginning of the mantle opening up.

The same key words that brought the fire from the chariots, God dwells inside the chariots of fire. "My Father, My Father! Behold the chariots of Israel and the horses thereof." That king who knew nothing because he wept. What opened it all was "weeping." Weeping comes before a miracle.

> *"Weeping may endure for a night, but joy co-*

*meth in the morning. I have hated the congre-*
*gation of evil doers; and will not sit with the*
*wicked. I will wash mine hands in innocency: so*
*will I compass thine altar, O Lord.*"
(Psalm 30:5b, 26:5 – 6)

Even though King Joash was a nobody who did not know God like the rest of us know God, God was ready to choose him because they that knew God had become leprous. Gehazi was the right candidate to take over but he had become leprous. In the day when God decides to choose you and finds you leprous, He will choose another man that you will look down on to take your place. You must be careful not to hand over the mantle to the man you have always despised. You will make somebody else qualify because you left your place, your duty post.

Do not let those great men of God die alone and carry away their anointing. Some of the men I saw God preparing to take over from Papa Adeboye are losing their place already. Some of them re getting out of the ministry while some have intentions to get out. If the old man that handed over to Papa Adeboye had not seen clearly, the ministry, the Church would not have been alive today. That is what kills men who have touched God before their time.

Katheryn Kuhlman said God transferred the anointing to her because the man that was supposed to carry the garment of the oil she was carrying refused, (even though he was still alive and doing Pentecostalism). God can take a stone and use it in your place. Do not ever think you are indispensable. I have never imagined that I am indispensable. God will just change you overnight and replace you with somebody else.

*"And when he was come nigh, even now at the*

*descent of the mount of Olives, the whole*

*multitude of the disciples began to rejoice and praise God with a loud voice for all the mighty works that they had seen; Saying, Blessed be the King that cometh in the name of the Lord: peace in heaven, and glory in the highest. And some of the Pharisees from among the multitude said unto him, Master, rebuke thy disciples. And he answered and said unto them, I tell you that, if these should hold their peace, the stones would immediately cry out"* (Luke 19:37 – 40).

Sometime membership will need to be patient with leadership. Otherwise, they would not receive the oil. There are times when leadership takes steps that seem wrong but eventually, they might become the source of salvation. Follow them gently in love. It is not the period to begin to cast and flog their oil. When you do that, you will be flogging your own oil. In heaven, you have disqualified yourself. When the people decided to go to Egypt and carry their gods, why did Jeremiah pack his load and follow them? He did it so that when they sought a man who would take them back to the Lord, he wanted to be there to carry them back. You must be careful: the thing you are helping to destroy now might become the source of salvation tomorrow. Do not help in destroying it.

# Personal Notes

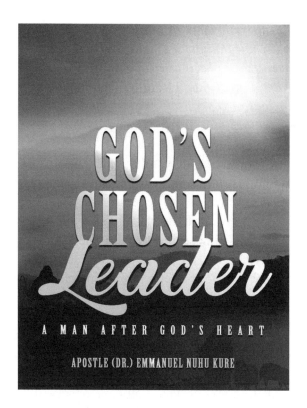

# CHAPTER 8

# Stop Grumbling!

There are people in the Church who are professional critics and love to grumble. The day the Pastor dances too much it will be the story throughout the day.

> *"Blessed is the man that walketh not in the counsel of the ungodly, nor standeth in the way of sinners, nor sitteth in the seat of the scornful.*

*But his delight is in the law of the Lord; and in his law doth he meditate day and night. And he shall be like a tree planted by the rivers of water, that bringeth forth his fruit in his season; his leaf also shall not wither; and whatsoever he doeth shall prosper"* (Psalm 1:1 – 3).

The person confronting may not have the guts to confront the Pastor. Yet he is grumbling to you so that your oil too can be smitten. The scornful do not necessarily need to be unbelievers. There are scornful in the church. This has destroyed a lot of churches. Sometimes, the story they tell is actually exaggerated and you work by an exaggerated anointing. You lay down your life and your integrity on the line for that exaggerated anointing.

God will mark you out as unqualified to carry the major oil. Why can't you get on your knees and pray? If God commands you or you saw it yourself, meet the man and tell him what the Lord has told you or what you have observed. If the man explains or says he saw or heard from God, then follow him gently because he too has said he saw from God. Since both of you have seen from God, who becomes the referee now? Allow God to judge the rest. Go back and take your place in the congregation and follow gently. If he calls God, it is God then. Do not abandon the place because it is possible the God who made you see is planting you there to become a salvation later. That is what happened to Jeremiah.

But the men of anointing we have these days are such that the pastor dares not make one mistake. That is why God goes the extra mile to hide the pastor from the congregation. The pastor makes mistakes except that you do not see. And may God never allow you to see because somebody is there to hang them and carry a coup. God hides them. Otherwise, you will manhandle them and destroy God's anointing to them.

But the man received the anointing that Elisha had received Verse 15 of 2 Kings 13 says Elisha told the king to take the bow and arrows and he did. And he said to the king of Israel to put his hand upon the bow and he did so. You see, he was teaching him how to open and release the anointing. Elisha put his hand upon the king's hands. Have I not told you that the hand is the doorway by which anointing is transferred? Have you not read in Habakkuk 3:4 that it is the palm of his hands. Therein lies the secret of his power. It flows like horns of fire. Elisha knew that the doorway of transferring the anointing on his head is his hands. But the man did not know. Having begun in the spirit, he did not see in the end.

Gehazi followed Elisha until the day he became too self-conscious and became leprous. The day you become too self-conscious, you will become leprous. The greatest men God used are the humblest men. The Bible says in understanding, be men.

**THE COUNSEL OF MEN**
The Bible says that after Elisha had finished instructing Joash and Elisha himself put his hand upon him (the king's hand), he said, "Open the window eastward." Did you notice that it was from the eastern gate that Ezekiel did something? God has been teaching me that from the east is the release of the breath of God. There is something about the east in the spiritual.

I notice a mystery that from the east is a mystery of the key of the breath of God that spreads around the earth to lay hold on the earth and make the earth do God's will. According to Isaiah 46:11, there is the Spirit of God that executes the counsel of God from the east. Why don't you sometimes face the east and say, "Oh God that dwells in the heavens, release the fountain of the east and let your life break the situation in my life by the power that dwells in the east in Jesus' name."

It will be like taking a mantle and hitting the river Jordan with it. When it touches the river Jordan, the river must break open. When you take the mantle like that from the east and hit the mountain, it must break.

I found out that when Daniel opened his windows towards Jerusalem, the place where his windows which he opened each time and faced Jerusalem – was facing east.

> *"Now when Daniel knew that the writing was signed, he went into his house; and his windows being open in his chamber toward Jerusalem, he kneeled upon his knees three times a day, and prayed, and gave thanks before his God, as he did aforetime"* (Daniel 6:10).

And Elisha told the king to shoot and he shot. Elisha saw the arrow of the Lord's deliverance and the arrows of deliverance from Syria. "For thou shall smite the Syrians in Aphet till thou has consumed them." If you read on, you will find that the king was foolish. At the end, he shot only three arrows. And Elisha said because the king failed to collect the anointing fully, he was afraid of the anointing; he was afraid to dare God. Therefore, he would smite his enemies only three times.

Immediately Elisha told him that, the Bible says Elisha died. He died of a heart attack because the last hope he had for the continuity of the anointing had just been dashed. There was no reason to live again, so he died.

## DO NOT JUDGE AFTER THE SIGHT
You will not judge after the sight. When men condemn others,

you will not join them. You will shut your mouth.

> *"And the spirit of the Lord shall rest upon him, the spirit of wisdom and understanding, the spirit of counsel and might, the spirit of knowledge and of the fear of the Lord; And shall make him of quick understanding in the fear of the Lord: and he shall not judge after the sight of his eyes, neither reprove after the hearing of his ears"* (Isaiah 11:2 – 3).

When you see a storm coming, you should not judge after the sight. When you see an accident come while driving, you will not judge after the sight. You will be reassured that you will come out of it unhurt. The natural sight ceases to be the interpretation, the spiritual sight becomes the real interpretation. You shall not judge after the hearing of the ear. When you say this brother hates you, you shall not judge after the hearing of the ear. Otherwise, you will be quick to making mistakes, and because of the anointing you carry, mistakes will be quick to destroy you.

I do not want to miss my chance and that is why I put cotton wool in my ears to stop noise from entering. If no man comforts me, I want to continue until the day I raise a call and none of you appears. Then I will know that the work has finished. The day I enter your city and everybody turns away, then I shall say, "Lord, now may your servant depart in peace" because my work is finished.

But until that day, the noise of men will not stop me. They may get me tiered sometimes. They may make me despair. I will not be the first. Paul despaired; Jeremiah despaired but the fire brought them back. I am preaching today because the fire has brought me back.

God said to me, "Have you resisted unto blood?" Has somebody put caterpillars before you? Until you allow somebody to do that, I shall not stop. If anybody does that, I will smash them to powder. I said, "God, it is not that I believe you, but the practice of it is difficult." Do I sound like somebody you know? Jeremiah said to God, "That is how you convinced me. But when the fire came, you disappeared. It was after I had finished eating mud that you appeared to say, "I am the Lord that healed thee. Where were you?" He complained that God had breached the agreement. Did He say you will not suffer?

Did God say there would be no tribulation or pain? Let me tell you, even though you walk through the shadow of the valley of death, He shall be there with you. At the end of the fire, you will be glorified. While the pain is there, it is not easy. But when it is over, it will be like the woman that has given birth. The joy of it shall overwhelm you.

> *"When thou passest through the waters, I will be with thee; and through the rivers, they shall not overflow thee: when thou walkest through the fire, thou shalt not be burned; neither shall the flame kindle upon thee. For I am the Lord thy God, the Holy One of Israel, thy Saviour: I gave Egypt for thy ransom, Ethiopia and Seba for thee. Since thou wast precious in my sight, thou hast been honourable, and I have loved thee: therefore will I give men for thee, and people for thy life"* (Isaiah 43:2 – 4).

Say, "Jesus, I honor you with my life, my substance, my everything. Where art thou? Now come to me my master. Come to my tabernacle. Accept me as I am. Break away the old man. I want a change of identity. I repent as Isaiah repented. My God, all my righteousness, all the sacrifice that I have done for you is like filthy rags compared to the glory you have given me. I want to taste of that fire. I want to taste of that burning. Come Jesus. I am ready to shake out the old self."

If the fire burns you, Isaiah 11:3 – 4 shall be fulfilled in your life.

> *"And shall make him of quick understanding in the fear of the Lord: and he shall not judge after the sight of his eyes, neither reprove after the hearing of his ears: But with righteousness shall he judge the poor, and reprove with equity for the meek of the earth: and he shall smite the earth with the rod of his mouth, and with the breath of his lips shall he slay the wicked."*

Your understanding shall come alive. You will no longer judge after the sight of your eyes for the weapons of the dragons has to do with the eyes. The weapons against the church has to do with the ears. Elijah climbed to Mount Carmel and closed his eyes while he prayed. Seven times he refused to see and yet he saw and he told another eye, "Go and check until you see what I am seeing." And while that man was checking, he was releasing lamps of fire within his bones to call what he sees. Let the counsel that sits in heaven hear my case before the twenty-four elders; before the mighty angels; before your mighty presence.

I appeal today that according to Revelation 22, flow into my life and make me pure. Open my life and restore my purity – my fruitfulness before you. Come Holy Ghost with the fire of the seven lamps that cometh from the throne – even the seven Spirits of God – let them step into my life. Let everything change from today. I shall not judge after the sight of the eyes or hearing of the ears but by the instruction by the Holy Spirit. Amen.

Stop Grumbling! 81

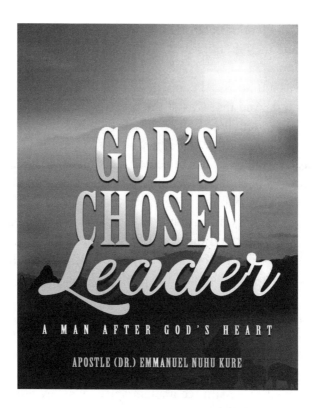

# CHAPTER 9

## Beware!

What is happening? It is like Israel has come to the place of birth, but she cannot give birth. Something must be wrong with the oil of Israel. The day of the oil of the Church has come, and it is like the Church does not know where to flow to any more. Rather than strength and glory, the Church has a deep fear over its head. There are many people today that are living in the fear of death. There is fear in the air, fear of many things, and they do not know how grace will come to finish it.

There was a time Israel came to a point of glory but could not enter into it. And that was at the time of Hezekiah, when Hezekiah had to rent his clothes and say, "This is the day of trouble." I want to say that the situation has come for the Church to re-assess and re-examine herself. It is time you checked the oil you have been using, whether or not it has been effective. It is time for every pastor to go and wear rags and ask the Lord where you have gone wrong in your prayers. Where have you smitten the water and the water was not healed? Where have you smitten the water wrongly? Where have you carried your battle against leviathan and the battle did not work?

What the church is up against this hour is the spirit and demon called leviathan. In Makurdi, I stood before a large crowd at IBB square. I saw leviathan come out from the sea. And I saw with it every strange ancient spirit that you can think of, and the leader of these strange ancient spirits was leviathan. That is what your oil is up against. And the spirit of leviathan is not only risen against this nation, it is risen against all the nations of the earth. Leviathan is risen so that it could release the plagues that will bring such confusion and tumult that would defy solution.

That means he is going to create situations that people cannot change in order to confuse economists. Americans are fighting their president. America is not comfortable and Iraq is not comfortable either. Everybody is not comfortable. It is the mystery of leviathan. Homes are being shaken by the same mystery of leviathan. People are acting irrationally and they cannot explain why they are doing so. There are irritations everywhere. Your neighbor in the market place does not know why he hates you. If you ask him, he cannot explain why.

There is just an irritation. The weather is so dry that the lives of people are being strangulated. As the sun is up and makes you uncomfortable, so do demons sit upon people's lives and make them uncomfortable. You get angry sometimes and do not know why you are angry. What is wrong?

The mystery of leviathan is at work. People are getting sick and there is no cure for their sickness. These days, may the doctors not soon get out of their professions because they now get more patients but they cannot really diagnose what is wrong with them. They keep guessing till the patient dies. Even the guessing is done in a pretense. This is why it is only the born-again doctors who are prayerful that are surviving the trade because by faith they can pray through and proffer solutions to the ailment.

It was reported over CNN that for almost every sickness now doctors have to look for new drugs to combat it because the old drugs are no longer effective. New malaria drugs are being manufactured because the old ones they know are failing. It has been reported by WHO that there are about thirty new emerging diseases now in the world, besides re-emerging ones.

The Lord showed me that leviathan has vomited out small snakes. What we are going through now is the mystery of the days of the serpent when in the wilderness serpents were released in judgment to smite and kill people with epidemic diseases. But the Lord said as many as will lift up their eyes to look at the golden snake would be saved. It means in this hour the Church has to withdraw and find out the golden snake, in order to save the people from the bite. Otherwise, Israel has come to the place of giving birth but it cannot give birth. It is a strange thing. The truth of the matter is that Nigeria is sick. The Church is sick. Everybody is sick. So it is time to look for the new curative drug that can knock out this sickness which seems to be defying every solution. It is time to withdraw and get the right medicines.

Elisha was not given to making noise; the fire from heaven spoke for him. The noise from heaven changed the situation, But because you are exerting your energy on things that do not matter, your oil is being taken from you. For some believers the day of their prophecy is over but they do not know it. The oil that you are showing off now is dead oil and you do not know. You think you are still alive.

What you need is to go back and ask for mercy so that God can restore you back to the days of grace. The days you had your chance you never used it. Instead, you used it to look for bread and butter. You used it for deceit instead of speaking against the affairs of this nation. I want you to put yourself in the place of your oil and I want you to judge yourself first, it is very vital. You know what happened in the days of Jehoshaphat and Ahab when some lying spirit entered into the mouth of the prophet and he said, "Go to war, it shall be well with you."

I see lying spirits and you should pray, "Oh God, let Macaiah arise, let the spirit of Macaiah come forth. Lying spirits must be stopped. They must not speak further through me. They must not kill or destroy my oil or the nation. Oh God, heal, Oh God deliver!" Pray, wrestle with God until your deliverance comes and you begin to face and fulfill the direction of God's calling and place for your life.

## THE OIL OF WITNESS
What God Almighty is waiting for now, and if there is anything the nation is groaning for now, is what are called "WITNESSES." Any oil that will be effective at this hour must be

the oil of witness. Whether you are a pastor or not, you must ask God to give you the oil of witness – not just any kind of oil – because that is the only one mystery that will stand against leviathan. And that is the oil of "witness." There is only one mystery that will stand before kings and stand before nations. It is the oil of witness. Some of you do not know you are ministers and that every minister is called of God, has physical ears, eyes, nose, mouth – but that in the spiritual he has a mechanism that is built over him.

In the story of Jacob, the Bible says there was a ladder from heaven that came straight to his head where he was laying his head. When he stood up, he said, "This must be the gate of heaven." But actually, the gate of heaven opened up to the altar of his heart. And that ladder came down up to his spirit and he saw angels descending from heaven to his spirit and ascending from his spirit to the havens.

Do you know that the day you become a minister there is a twenty-four hour transmission of the life and spirit and fellowship with God. There is a twenty-four hour transmission, whether you are conscious of it or not. Even when you are tired, it is on. When you are not in tune, it is on. If it is removed, you are dead. If it is removed for once, the devil will avenge all the havoc you have caused his kingdom by your obedience to God.

Do you know that even in backsliding, that an altar still stands for you. The altar does not leave or you are dead. That is why you will notice something in Revelation chapter 11, which are called witnesses, and the spiritual name where their bodies laid for three days is called Sodom and Egypt. But do you know that the spiritual abode for their bodies, for their souls, for their physical bodies is a candlestick?

As a priest, you are a candle. In Revelation 11:18, the church is referred to as a candlestick. There were seven candlesticks and Jesus walked around them. That is the spiritual name for everyone that carries the oil of the Lord. I am a candlestick. You are a candlestick. If you look at Zechariah 4, Zerubabel is called a candlestick, but there the description is a little bit more. In Revelation 11, the Bible says there were trees. Each candlestick had a tree hidden in it with oil. The tree that stands over you will not give you over to death anyhow.

> *"And I will give power unto my two witnesses, and they shall prophesy a thousand two hundred and threescore days, clothed in sackcloth. These are the two olive trees, and the two candlesticks standing before the God of the earth. And if any man will hurt them, fire proceedeth out of their mouth, and devoureth their enemies: and if any man will hurt them, he must in this manner be killed"* (Revelation 11:3 – 4).

We are not an ordinary human being. So when an herbalist comes boasting over your life, tell him your life is not ordinary. He cannot take your life anyhow. Your life is worth more than that. The existence of your life is hidden in the existence of God Almighty.

> *"If ye then be risen with Christ, seek those things which are above, where Christ sitteth on the right hand of God. Set your affection on things above, not on things on the earth"* (Colossians 3:1 – 2).

## YOU ARE AN OLIVE TREE
Each time God looks at you, he sees an olive tree. As a priest, you are an olive tree – you are an oil. If you are a minister that the Lord has separated and ordained, what God has done is

to gather your oil together and make it one tree. It means you have been made an olive tree. And that is why the balm we pour is important. The Bible says that they were olive trees and candlesticks before the Lord their God. There were the two olive trees and the two candlesticks standing before the God of the earth. Do you note that covenant name, "God of the earth?" The mission of those two olive trees was for the earth, not for the heavens. So, the God of the earth ensured that the two olive trees spoke to the earth and the earth heard them.

In this hour of your life, God has to become the God of the earth. The Bible says he sets up kings and he brings them down, The Bible says God controls the economy of the nations. It means your oil is supposed to be geared toward healing nations, healing the economy, healing situations because you are a covenant candlestick. The Bible says,

> "And if any man will hurt them, fire proceedeth out of their mouth, and devoureth their enemies: and if any man will hurt them, he must in this manner be killed. These have power to shut heaven, that it rain not in the days of their prophecy: and have power over waters to turn them to blood, and to smite the earth with all plagues, as often as they will."
> (Revelation 11:5 – 6)

Do you know why? It is because these two witnesses never saw themselves as ordinary human beings. They allowed the consciousness of the fact that they were olive trees and candlesticks to control them. Zechariah tells us more,

> "And said unto me, What seest thou? And I said, I have looked, and behold a candlestick

Beware!                                                89

*all of gold, with a bowl upon the top of it, and*
*his seven lamps thereon, and seven pipes to the*
*seven lamps, which are upon the top thereof:*
*And two olive trees by it, one upon the right*
*side of the bowl, and the other upon the left side*
*thereof"* (Zechariah 4:2 – 3).

In the case of Zechariah, he had two olive trees feeding one
candlestick. In Revelation 11, each one of them was an olive
tree and a candlestick. It is a mystery.

Your oil flows according to the role that God has ordained for
you to fulfill on earth. No matter how you beg for extra oil,
it will not be added because that is not the role that has been
ordained for you. Zechariah was ordained to bring back the
glory of the latter house what no ordinary human being could
bring back. God had to station two olive trees. It is like an en-
gine with two fuel tanks to pour the oil upon the candlestick.
That was to bring the glory of the latter house. It means it was
to lift up the ordinances of kings and reverse everything the
ancient spirits have done.

A look at Revelation 11 shows that these men were supposed
to be the last witnesses on earth before the final judgment
comes. And instead of trees staying in heaven and feeding one
person, God made them to become the trees themselves on
earth. They were as it were still the candlesticks. That means
the oil by itself spoke directly not just empowering the candlesticks. Even when your enemies die in most cases, you do not
go about laughing anyhow if you are a normal human being.
Anybody you see laughing over the death of his enemy is abnormal. He needs deliverance.

God knows that these peope were going to face human beings
that were equal to demon incarnates. This serpent that levia-

than has vomited out has possessed them and was using them to sting and sting further. So, it means that this oil that God is raising in these people will have to answer back to those serpent spirits. That is why they themselves have to become oil. Your calling and the role you ought to play decides the oil that is ordained unto you. It decides the orientation of that oil. Every minister must find his place of oil because many ministers want to act the office that is not their own.

If you have jumped into ministry without knowing the area of your calling and you are already holding a position and a calling that you are not too comfortable with, you had better go back to your ministry or senior Pastor and tell him to reassign you to office work. A calling become a calling when it bears fruit and calls people into the kingdom. Anything short of this makes the calling a failure.

Philip started by serving tables and he operated in the same anointing, even more than Paul. Elisha started by carrying bags but manifested a higher anointing than Elijah. Today you will quarrel over that. Everybody wants to be a bishop and have his own empire. Nobody wants to serve tables to get the anointing. Yet therein lies the secret of anointing and receiving direction in ministry. Remember, the thing you look down upon might be the key to your oil. Go back to serving tables and you will come back alive.

I know many ministers may misconceive this. They will wonder why they would have to go back to the stage of serving tables again as a sign of withdrawal for their eyes to see clearly and catch a fresh vision of God without the former hindrance of their former high position. It is like withdrawing to the place where you will be yourself without any competition or anybody to compare yourself with and be content to learn only from God without distraction. This alone scripturally is the key to restoring you back to God's predestined plan for your life.

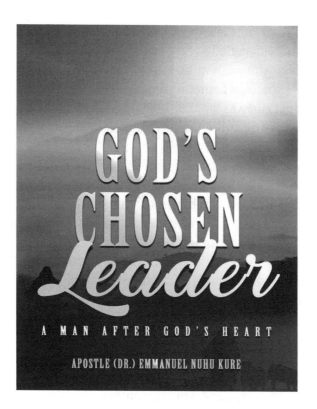

# CHAPTER 10

## Your Labor Is For A Day

If you look at the parable of the laborers, some were employed in. the morning, some in the afternoon while some were employed at six o'clock in the evening. At the end, they were all paid the same amount of money.

Notice that the time you have on earth to work is one day. Your whole life on earth is equal to one day. Even if you live for fifty years, it is one day. It is one day's work you are doing. You have been called to do one day's work. It does not matter at what age you get born-again or what time you answered the call for laborers, whether it is one year of your life on earth or you started early as a child. It is the same one day's work and the same pay according to faithfulness.

You have not yet started living on earth. Living on earth is after the one day's work. After the one day's work, you will begin to live forever. What you are doing on earth is not what God planned originally when he made man. God planned that man would live with him forever. There was to be no death, no breaking off for a while. There was to be no timing for judgment, timing for scrutiny, etc. There was to be no break. When God made Adam and Eve, they were to live forever with God. Sin brought the beginning of the one day. And after one day, eternity will begin again.

The end of your work is the night. That means what you have to fight towards, what you are up against is the night. The night must not catch you unawares. Hear what Jesus said,

> *"I must work the works of him that sent me, while it is day: the night cometh, when no man can work. As long as I am in the world, I am the light of the world"* (John 9:4 – 5).

My business for the day is to be the light of the world. He said, "I must work the works of him that sent me." Notice that when Jesus worked on the man who was born blind, he spat on the ground, made mud with the spittle and put it on the man's eyes (the work the father sent him to do). The father sent him to take care of human beings.

Are you going to sit there and allow situations to determine your actions? Or has God already ordained you into an action? Do you wait for the wind to make you act? Or is there an action God has put in your heads that He wants you to carry through? Is it not what God has pre-ordained over your life that you carry out? It is when you begin to carry it out that the wind that comes against you is taken care of.

God has ordained me into a mission. He has given me a focus. My business is to carry out that focus. When you establish your focus, it will confront the wind. It will deal with the wind that comes against you. The reason the wind is tossing you to and fro is because you are not carrying out that thing which God ordained you to do. Your focus is broken, you do not have a direction. So, the wind decides your direction. Today, you must make up your mind so that the wind does not decide your direction. You are to work against the wind. But when you find the wind blowing in your direction then, praise the Lord, work together with it.

Many of us do not have a direction because the wind dictates our directions and our actions, not the calling of God in our lives. God has anointed you to set the captives free. Whether the environment is conducive for you to set the captives free or not, you must set them free. You must not go back to farming or to the office again. He has called you out. The job must be done because you only have a day to give account for your life.

Some of you have a destiny. The reason why God would punish you in heaven is because you did not fulfill your destiny. **Your MEAT must be to DO the will of Him that sent you and to finish His WORK.** You must do and finish it. And you have only a day to finish it. Your business is to fight against the time to finish the work.

There is no service anyhow. Every calling and service the Lord releases is to fulfill a thing. Until you fulfill that thing and finish it, you have no reason to die. Anyone who dies without finishing his work must beg for his life. "God give me that life again, let me live and fulfill your work." In the day you rise to fulfill God's will, whether you like it or not, you may suffer for a while. But at the end, goodness and mercy will follow you.

> "Therefore, my beloved brethren, be ye stedfast, unmoveable, always abounding in the work of the Lord, forasmuch as ye know that your labour is not in vain in the Lord."
> (1 Corinthians 15:58).

Make up your mind. Be clear of the vision God has given you and rise to fulfill it.

## LAY DOWN YOUR LIFE

> "Hereby perceive we the love of God, because he laid down his life for us: and we ought to lay down our lives for the brethren" (1 John 3:16).

If you are a minister, you have been called to lay down your life for the brethren. Your business for that one day is to lay down your life for others. You have no business holding it back. He called you to look like Him, to carry His priesthood. Lay down your life and hold back nothing. That is what is expected of you. That is the pattern God has left for you. When you work, you are happy doing it. You are not constrained to do it. It is not a luxury calling. It is your work. Do not expect any appreciation for what is expected of you. If your life is not laid down for the brethren, the love of God is not in you whether you are a leader or not.

Every man that Jesus got born again is sent out. Every fruit of Jesus is in turn sent out.

> *"I must work the works of him that sent me, while it is day: the night cometh, when no man can work. As long as I am in the world, I am the light of the world. When he had thus spoken, he spat on the ground, and made clay of the spittle, and he anointed the eyes of the blind man with the clay, And said unto him, Go, wash in the pool of Siloam, (which is by interpretation, Sent.) He went his way therefore, and washed, and came seeing"* (John 9:4 – 7).

Every fruit God brings to your life must in turn be sent out. You must orient the fruit to go out. It was the power of God in that sputum that brought healing in those eyes. But why did he say, "Go wash in the pool of Siloam"? What is the meaning of Siloam in this case? Because it was in the pool of Siloam that his ordination will take place. It was there that the blind would receive the oil to be like Jesus so he can be sent. The problem with most of you is that when you got born again, you never washed in Siloam.

Some of you should begin to say, "Father, let me go, loosen me." Your zeal is not that of a person who has been released yet. Even when Jesus has touched you, until you wash in the river, the inspiration to go will not come. You will notice that the man had to wash in Siloam before he became a witness. He did not need to struggle to witness. People were magnetically attached to him. All he knew was, "Once I was blind, but now I see." The more they told him to shut up, the more he witnessed Jesus, "Once I was blind, now I see." He became "Sent." It was in Siloam that he received his release.

Some of you need the "Siloam" experience. When you are released, all of you is released. Your character is released. When your character is still living contrary to God's word, it means you have not been released. When those habits chain you down and make you displease God every day, it means you have not been released. Until you become "Sent," you are not complete in Christ yet.

When you give birth to a child, it normally looks like you (the parent). Jesus touched you, but you do not look like him. Something is wrong somewhere. You will notice something. One is touching and the other is washing. It is He that touches you but you do the washing. So, the act of washing it carried out by the individual that is touched. That means, you must willingly seek Him and allow Him to release you. The first thing is that He seeks you and heals you. But the second thing is that you too should seek Him and allow Him to release you.

How does He release you? When He begins to wipe out your character that is no longer proper. The majority of those who call themselves born again belong to the first side of being touched by the Lord – not Siloam. Their cycle is not complete yet. They need to wash in Siloam and look like God. The day you are born again and wash in Siloam, you too will become "Sent."

When you become "sent," you become a pilgrim. That Siloam experience does not come until you rise up to "work out your salvation with fear and trembling." You must go through the full cycle, a touch and a Siloam experience. In every congregation, every member must be "Sent." Every member must be a succor to the other. Jesus was a succor to people. Our congregation must be geared toward this. Otherwise, we have not completed the cycle.

All the people who are leading must be sent. If you do not bring them to that level, you are not successful yet. **They should all operate as a people with a mission and a people on a mission.**

You can only come against the wind according to that which the Lord has ordained you to carry out. It is with that you go through the day. Because you are sent, now you can operate in the day before it is night according to the sending whereby you have been sent. So every single individual will live a fulfilled life. When your night comes, you will give a good smile and say, "I have fought the good fight. I am ready to go." If you die without fulfilling your destiny, you are in trouble.

There is an anointing that is called "Sent." You must have a sense of responsibility toward that. Become "Sent" and then every wind that comes against you has to contend with that word "SENT."

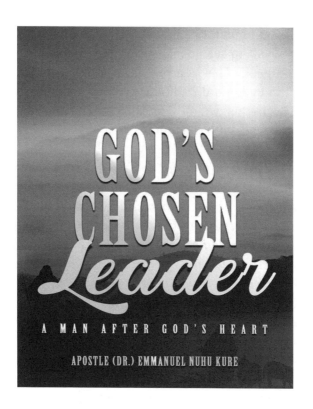

# CHAPTER 11

## Sodomic Spirit And Warfare

The spirit of Sodom and Egypt killed the Lord Jesus Christ. It was the spirit of Sodom and Egypt that killed those two witnesses. It is the same spirit of Sodom and Egypt that can give the Church a tough time in the day of the coming of the Lord. What is the spirit of Sodom and Egypt? It is the reprobate spirit. When the Bible says you have developed a reprobate mind, it means your mind is not only evil, but it does not understand good. For that mind, evil is good. His good is to do wickedness. He wants to see people suffer. He has lost the power to appreciate good. That is a reprobate mind: one whose mind is turned to evil and does not appreciate good anymore. It is like he was born a demon. The Bible in Romans, chapter one describes people with such minds:

> *"And even as they did not like to retain God in their knowledge, God gave them over to a reprobate mind, to do those things which are not convenient; Being filled with all unrighteousness, fornication, wickedness, covetousness, maliciousness; full of envy, murder, debate, deceit, malignity; whisperers, Backbiters, haters of God, despiteful, proud, boasters, inventors of evil things, disobedient to parents, Without understanding, covenant breakers, without natural affection, implacable, unmerciful: Who knowing the judgment of God, that they which commit such things are worthy of death, not only do the same, but have pleasure in them that do them"* (Romans 1:28 – 32).

In the days of Sodom and Gomorrah, it was when they fornicated, they felt they were enjoying life. They were not only fornicating, they were also involved in homosexual practices and in beast sex: dogs having sex with human beings. Do you know that snakes now have sex with human beings? The Bible calls it inordinate affection. That was the sin of Sodom and Gomorrah and that sin was founded in cultism: cult, Satanism and rituals.

In the day when you see rituals becoming the order of the day, then know that we are getting onto the sin of Sodom and Gomorrah. In that day, the anointing of the church will be resisted to death. So when the Lord is talking about the sin of Sodom, he is talking about people with a sodomic orientation. There is no good in their tongues. All they know is evil. The more good you do, the more somebody gets angry. He must kill you. It means he has a sodomic spirit. Bind that spirit and cast it out of your way. It is the strange spirit that attempts to overcome the greatest anointing.

The two witnesses had the anointing to hold the rains when they felt like. But a sodomic spirit brought them down and killed them.

Before the spirit of Sodom becomes powerful around you, begin to cut if off. There is a spirit of Sodom you must watch out for. It is the spirit that sees good as evil and will resist that good. So it means you never appeal to the conscience of the person, and he can never have mercy on you. He is just determined to kill you no matter what you do for him.

You can have people with that spirit in your family. You can have them as your immediate brother or sister. You can have them as your uncles, as your schoolmates, etc. Watch out! Do not spare them because they will not repent. No diplomacy will bring them to your side. No matter what you do, they will not see it until they kill you.

What should you do? Draw your sword and cut them. Try to cut them or move away from them before they cut you off because you did not stop them. They are the only ones who cannot admire your oils. This is what you will be contending against in these last days. The devil is manufacturing them, preparing them for the day of the persecution of the Church and for the war against Christ. So their specie are being born now and gradually being released. It is time to rise up against the spirit of Sodom.

When you hear God still making reference to Egypt like this, it means Egypt has not repented. This present-day Egypt has not repented. It will still carry out evil against Israel. But right now, it is like the most harmless country. It will become the thorn. Egypt and Israel have lived together. But do not underestimate the quietness of Egypt. The Bible says it was that spirit that hung Jesus on the cross.

If it could succeed to take the master that came down and hung him on the cross, how much less you? It took a cry in heaven for an earthquake to settle it. That is why God says the only anointing that is going to work in these last days is the devouring anointing. He says, "I will visit you with an earthquake, lightning and fire."

You must take the spirit of Sodom by the root and disarm it. Clear it. Take it out of the way quickly! If he is your own brother, sister, uncle, etc., please take him or her out of the way. Otherwise, you will be in serious trouble. The practical solution is, TAKE THEM OUT OF THE WAY! And when they are arch enemies, then release earthquakes. They have to be removed.

By prayer, rise up and take a song that makes God sit on his throne. And once He sits on the throne, ask Him to release the angels of war against those enemies or things. Let Him sit over your situations and let Him go to war with you. You need to know how to go to war with God. Do not be lazy when coming into His presence. Make Him go to war as King of kings.

I like the way the Yorubas in Nigeria went to war in their day. They used to go to war in fanfare. The drummers were beating, stirring up each man of war, singing his praises and charging him up. If you want to go to war, put God on the throne and go to war. See how King Jehoshaphat knew the mystery of stirring God's jealousy.

> *"And Jehoshaphat stood in the congregation of Judah and Jerusalem, in the house of the Lord, before the new court, And said, O Lord God of our fathers, art not thou God in heaven? and rulest not thou over all the kingdoms of the heathen? and in thine hand is there not power and might, so that none is able to withstand thee? Art not thou our God, who didst drive out the inhabitants of this land before thy people Israel, and gavest it to the seed of Abraham thy friend forever?"* (2 Chronicles 20:5 – 7)

The Bible records that after stirring God's emotion, he ordered that singers should walk in the front of the warriors of Judah and Jerusalem, singing praise unto God and because God's jealousy was stirred, He caused confusion among the invaders of Israel. Their enemies killed themselves and the children of Israel only went in to pack the booties.

Release earthquakes and the spirit of Sodom will disappear. You must learn how to survive the times. Call for the review of our battle strategy.

**THE DAY OF YOUR PROPHECY**
If in the book of Revelation, Egypt is still mentioned, then there is a mystery about Egypt that will continue to the end of the age.

> *"And their dead bodies shall lie in the street of the great city, which spiritually is called Sodom and Egypt, where also our Lord was crucified."*
> (Revelation 11:8)

Notice what verse six says,

*"These have power to shut heaven, that it rain not in the days of their prophecy: and have power over waters to turn them to blood, and to smite the earth with all plagues, as often as they will"* (Revelation 11:6).

Note that every anointing has its day of manifestation. So every one called of God has his days of prophecy. Are you a business man? Your riches have their days of expression. When those days pass, your riches will become irrelevant. Do not miss the day of the expression of your riches. Otherwise, you will not come to the peak of your life. Are you a man of God procrastinating and thinking you have time? During the time you have now, let your oil speak. Your oils have set days of prophecy. Let the night not come on your oils. Do you know that the days of your prophecy can be over before your die? The Bible showed that Daniel's of prophecy finished before he died.

"But go thou thy way till the end be: for thou shalt rest, and stand in thy lot at the end of the days" (Daniel 12:13).

When he finished prophesying and being relevant on the people he was supposed to, the Lord called him to go and take the place he would want to the day of his rest, meaning that Daniel had shown all those anointings during his days. But before he died, he had to shut up. He had not heard again, He rested.

Know also that Paul in the New Testament finished his work but did not die immediately. He rested before he died. You may still be relevant to the church. But your oil may not speak as sharply as it needed to in your days of prophecy. Some other people must have taken over your oil. So it is not necessary that it must be death that will stop your last flow.

But please note that it is also possible for God to retire you before the night comes, that is before the day of your rest comes. William Seymour was retired before the day of his rest. Kathryn Kuhlman also almost went through the path of Seymour. The days of Pa Benson Idahosa had passed before the day of his rest – before he was called home. He was kept alive for a while because there was one or two more things that the Lord wanted him to relevantly raise a standard for. Elisha's days of prophecy had finished before he died. He had some days of rest. Actually, if you have served God faithfully, He will give you not only long life, but He also give you the one for rest so that you can see the travail of your soul and be satisfied.

These are days and years of strange anointing. Every minister must mind his righteousness. He must be careful to make sure he builds according to the pattern shown him. The days of your prophecy are limited. You only have one day. Have the days you have spent so far in ministry been meaningful? Pray the oil never forsakes you because the day it domes, you are finished. Do not allow God to retire you before your time and do not retire yourself.

Are the days of your prophecy wasted? Are the oils still speaking? Has the night come over your life? To what usefulness is your oil? How do you know whether the night has come already on your oils?

## PROPHECY MUST BE FULFILLED
Prophecy must be fulfilled. The Bible must be fulfilled. There is a baptism of fire – an anointing of fire is catching up with the people; that is beginning to consume the people. That baptism is not only destroying the rest of the flesh, but every limitation of the flesh as well as any form of backsliding. Hopeless

and impossible situations are being broken. They are being reversed.

Will you awake one day ad hear somebody ask you, "Did you say something?" He will come to ask you repeatedly. The encounter between Eli and Samuel would be repeated in this age. It would be experienced in a greater dimension. When you hear that voice, note that the Spirit of God is speaking to you.

In those days of mighty miracles and great evangelistic out-reaches, when anointing came upon great men of God, a whole factory was brought to a standstill. It was recorded in the history of Wesleyan revivals that as he stepped into the factory one day, the first person who sighted him thought he heard Wesley say, "Repent, you are a sinner. You are doomed to hell."

Conviction and the reality of an eternity in hell dawned on him. The perception of the great God standing on him came upon him. The man was just visiting without uttering a word. It was the gift of God in him that began to convict the person of sin. Henceforth, anyone who say the visitor, stopped work-ing, and in the twinkling of an eye, the whole factory was crying repentance.

We are going to witness this kind of anointing these coming years. We shall experience many forms of resurrection. By your hands, people will rise from the dead. There will be such bold faith inside you that would insist that this situation must turn around. You will stamp your feet until there is a break-through.

This kind of anointing has started in Kafanchan. The Lord has blessed us with men who are growing in faith even while the ministry was going through a traumatic period in 1997 – 98. They covered the nakedness here. Otherwise, there would not have been a ministry today. In spite of the darkness, the turmoil and the confusion the ministry was being dragged into, they were waxing stronger. They went into hiding where they derived their strength. They had learned that the secret of their strength came from the Most High. As a result of their withdrawal, they asked God to stop the rains on the days of our night vigils, and God was faithful. They asked God to overlook the infirmity of the ministry since there was a glory that was going and it had to continue. It means the right orientation is catching up with us – a right orientation that would bring rain, a spiritual rain, a harvest that would begin from Kafanchan.

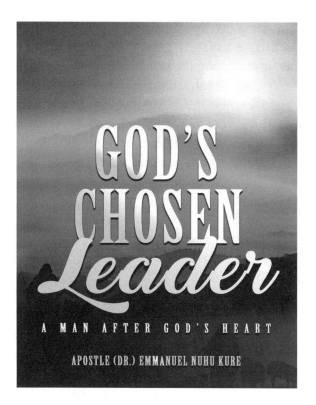

# CHAPTER 12

## The Pulpit

The pulpit is the minister's Mount Zion. It is a sacred, consecrated place where the Lord comes down to the people. It represents the place of the dwelling of the altar. And where the altar of sacrifice dwells, the Lord dwells there. That is why the pulpit is also referred to as the ALTAR, the place where God hovers, where He dwells within the church, where He ministers from. It is sacred. The supernatural flows from there.

Every minister must watch over his pulpit. He must keep it sacred, sanctify it always, renew its covenant of life with God often, and pray it through to heaven as the place of miracles. If you do this often, the miraculous will never depart from there. Even in your absence, the presence of the Lord you have covenanted there by your prayer, praise and covenant sacrifices between you alone will release the supernatural life of God on those who kneel before God at the altar.

The altar is the place of the presence of God, the place of the seven Spirits of God. It is the site of the throne of God from where He judges the people and they in turn reach out to Him in fellowship. It is from there that the supernatural reaches out to the people in His tongues of fire.

> *"And out of the throne proceeded lightnings and thunderings and voices: and there were seven lamps of fire burning before the throne, which are the seven Spirits of God."*
> (Revelation 4:5)

A brother my name Joshua, after bearing 10 years of spite and mockery for childlessness by people and relatives, was driven by desperation. One night, after our meetings, he and his wife laid on their faces at our Gethsemane Prayer Camp. They laid themselves on the holy altar, anointed themselves with oil and formed a ring of oil around themselves and cried all night that their reproach be taken away from them. The God of altars broke the curse from that night. Of course, we might have stopped them from using the altar that way. But the Lord saw their faith and desperation and answered them from the altar. Joshua and his wife today are staff in the ministry with a big boy to show for it. Altars speak. Make your own altar to speak for you.

You must sanctify yourself before you climb the pulpit. Always, the last minute before I climb the pulpit anywhere, I go to the throne of grace one final time and I asked Him passionately NOT to let me go out to that pulpit alone because I did not call myself.

I ask Him to release me, to pour the oil of that meeting on my head that second without which I cannot go. I tell Him it is Him the people want to see and hear, not me. And it is Him alone that melts their burdens always. I do not want to interfere. I beg Him to let us settle any case He might have against me for the hungry peoples' sake. Sometimes, I weep when I am in this position on my knees or with my face bowed just before the pulpit.

But in all cases, I feel helpless and trapped and subject to His mercy and whatever He does with me and his people that are waiting. I stay like that praying and pleading for the oil until I feel or hear Him pouring that sacred oil of release and mercy on my head, or in my heart.

Even then on my way to the pulpit, I still feel frightened and not sure. Somehow, it happens almost every time. I have never been very sure of myself in any sermon. I wait on the Holy Spirit to manipulate my feelings, my revelations and my understanding. When He is not doing it, I am frightened and insecure and unsure of myself.

Strangely, after going through all these, immediately when I climb the pulpit, something happens to me. I cannot explain it. It's like something slips out of my personality. Kure loses control. A divine energy, a life I cannot explain goes through my whole body. I feel light. The voice changes. It becomes a voice of compelling authority and power. Not imposed authority or made-up authority or theatrics or pulpit antics. I just feel captured by a power that seems to have always been on that pulpit waiting for me. I feel transfigured. It subjects my will and compels me all through. It is then that the fear and anxiety about that message disappears.

You must withdraw to discover the spiritual patterns of God with you. You have no right representing Him if you cannot discover His dwelling and His pattern for your life. He has a pattern for every minister. The results are always the same. You become swallowed in Him when it comes to representing Him before the people. The results will flow effortlessly, and the fruits of your labor will begin to pour out. Otherwise, you will end up seeking yourself, your wisdom, the things you learnt from school only and not what He taught you, and your emptiness will in turn scatter rather then keep. The letter kills but the spirit gives life.

There are many time I have to anoint myself in desperation with oil at the last minutes before a message – such times when I need a resurrection of His presence and hand upon me. At that time, I feel a hold come on me. I feel a mandate, a reassurance that I am sent and not on my own. Sometimes this happens in the car. Sometimes just before I get out of the house or hotel for the pulpit, I fall on my face to ask for a mandate or to be sent out. I always want to be and feel sent for every message so that God can take responsibility for all that happens afterwards.

Anoint your head whenever you do not feel confident and secure behind the altar of God. It brings you under God's cover while you preach. It is the physical contact between the oils in heaven and your life. It is the assurance of the finger of that oil in the olive "trees" in heaven on you.

Such times immediately, I climb the pulpit I feel a strange

bond and a transmission of God's Spirit flow through me as a current. Then I know that whatever I do, I am not responsible. He has taken over to do all things to please Himself and fulfill His work and will on earth.

There are other ministers who, to assuage their hunger and to assure themselves of God's presence, eat the flesh and drink the blood of Jesus in a holy communion between them and the Lord alone. This renews the bond of priesthood that binds the Lord and them together. This involves the renewal and establishment of the flow of the fellowship and the priest. Every priest should once and a while break bread alone between him and the Most High God and stay in communion in His presence.

When you break bread this way, you are renewing and building an altar. You are building a Jacob's ladder for fellowship. You are opening a door (a gate) of heaven, the fellowship of Revelation 8:5 – 6 and your person. It is a fellowship between priests.

Have you not read that Jesus is the priest in his sanctuary which is you? He is the priest over the house of God.

> *"We have such an high priest, who is set on the right hand of the throne of the Majesty in the heavens; A minister of the sanctuary, and of the true tabernacle, which the Lord pitched, and not man... Having therefore, brethren, boldness to enter into the holiest by the blood of Jesus, By a new and living way, which he hath consecrated for us, through the veil, that is to say, his flesh; And having an high priest over the house of God"* (Hebrews 8:1 – 2; 10:19- 21).

When you break bread as a priest (above) between you and God, you are establishing an altar of fellowship in your soul and invoking the minister of that altar – Jesus – to minister inside of you. Try it and see the wonderful fellowship that opens up between you and God.

Many time I have been in the pulpit and seen the Spirit of the Lord ministering to the people and showing me exactly the things He is doing on them. I know when He is grieved and when He is lifted away. It is like I am in another presence and being made to do what they are doing there.

The pulpit for me is a fellowship experience. A fellowship between me and the Holy Spirit. I hear myself being told things and find myself doing them naturally. The pulpit for you should be a place of fellowship between you and God. There you can call down fire. It is the holiest place of covenant in the sanctuary. It is the power place, the place of sacrifice. It should be hallowed and sanctified ALWAYS. It is where the minister completely becomes swallowed by his God. It is the seat of God in the sanctuary. The minister that hallows it shall be hallowed. He knows God's presence. A minister daily needs to sanctify himself every time even when he is sure he is clean before he climbs it. There he becomes invisible. He loses his presence in the presence of God. The seven flames of fire reaches out from there, NOT the minister.

The congregation should ALWAYS judge this by the word. No matter what God says or does must AGREE with the Holy Scriptures. They do not bring a cloud, depression or fear on the congregation even when they agree with the word of God. They bring liberation. If whatever is happening from the pulpit is not liberating your spirit, it is NOT from God no matter who the minister behind that oil is – no matter his importance or the respect you have for him. Judge every spirit every time and each time and as many times as they appear in the pulpit.

Never get too used to an oil. Otherwise, you won't know when heresy comes in. And do not jump to causing a riot because the church and the Lord will hold you responsible. If they are minor flips, let go and pray more for your minister. There is no minister on earth who never goes through flips. Where there are deliberate heresies, take scriptural steps to check them. Do not be erratic or emotional about it. Intense emotions becloud sanity and therefore, leads to many mistakes even in a righteous cause. BEWARE!

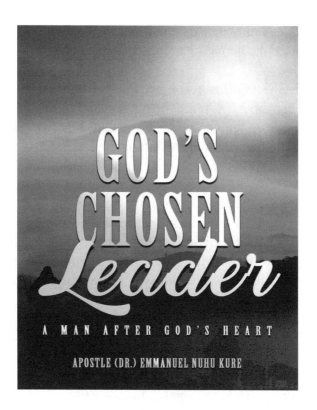

# CHAPTER 13

# The Spiritual Marriage Bond

*"We know that we have passed from death unto life, because we love"* (1 John 3:14).

Marriage is an altar of fellowship between God and man. The right couple (Marriage) instituted and ordained by God is a channel of the flow of fellowship between God and man. They enjoy such warmth and fellowship of the Spirit between them that no man can break. By their altar and fellowship, God is made rea. to the humanity around them.

Marriage is God's channel of meeting. He enforces one by one so that His wholeness might be made manifest. The fusion of two into one is the combined force that is capable of making the gospel unbreakable and invincible. It is the power that breaks every wall and makes the gospel live forever.

We know that the Holy Spirit does everything. It is the creative power of God on earth that makes all things possible. The woman is the creative oil of God that makes the man's fulfillment in ministry possible. She is an empowering factor in the man's life. Take her away and the husband's ministry will never be fully accomplished. She gives the ministry its glory and puts the man in the place of favor – favor with God and with man. This is the first major accomplishment of the oil of the woman in the man's life.

A minister's wife is his shield. Take her away and the minister, no matter how anointed will amount to nothing. Once people know you are married, they look at you with respect. The woman in your life by divine arrangement is God's covenant of favor with you. She is the signet of God. She is God's promises of favor for you.

*"Whoso findeth a wife findeth a good thing, and obtaineth favour of the Lord"* (Proverbs 18:22).

So she can become your making or unmaking. You as the man must take pains to learn how to control her oil. Otherwise, your ministry will lose direction or impact. God ordained her oil to establish you and not to destroy you. She is your spiritual completeness, the final shield of protection over you in the spiritual.

For every minister, no marriage is a mistake. Search carefully, you will find that God's divine finger is in it somewhere in order to establish the divine purpose he planned your life to accomplish for Him. She might not eventually be the specifications of the demand of your spirit or flesh (she often does not), but she was planted deliberately by the Holy Spirit in your life to help you accomplish the particular purpose he fitted you to fulfill. So your choice (likes or dislikes in a wife) may not necessarily be what God gives you in order to fulfill His will. This is a mystery every minister must either be willing to face and accept, or kick against and fall out of God's plan.

Jacob in his heart labored for Rachel. But Leah was God's choice for his life. That is why Leah was buried in the sepulcher of Jacob's fathers with Jacob but Rachel was not. She had two children. But the will of Jacob did not go far in bearing fruit – children.

Your marriage will take you far in accomplishing God's work. Don't push it or you will find yourself going in circles or striving in ministry rather than breaking ground. There is a divine pattern even in marriage that accomplishes God's work. Your life can only fulfill it by that pattern or lose out when you impose upon it. You are either accepting and flowing in it completely or not flowing at all.

All women are God's signets of divine favor (covenant rainbow) over men. All women are oils and carry oils, and are capable of manifesting the power in the oil.

## MARRIAGE AS A CALLING
The Lord God Almighty joins people together in marriage according to the calling and orientation he created in them when he made them.

An Abrahamic calling (the man with Apostolic callings) has a Sarah anointing to cover it and make it complete. A Deboraic calling (a woman with apostolic calling) has some kind of equivalent anointing in the husband as Sarah to make it complete. There is also the Nabal calling (the fool yet gifted) and the Abigailic (wise and intelligent) for a wife to make or cover complete. Without an Abigail, a Nabal will die or never be fulfilled. And lastly, the Acquilla callings (men with evangelical anointing) and a Priscilla (women with like fires and emotions) as cover. God never makes mistakes in choosing two partners (husband and wife) for His work. Every leader and minister's marriage falls into one of these categories.

Find your own. God never makes mistakes in choosing, bonding one man to one woman from different parents and orientations. It is deliberate to fulfill His will. Your marriage is not a mistake no matter what your present circumstances are. If you do not know how to relate to the oil of your wife, it will affect the direction and accomplishments of your ministry. You must learn how to relate with the oil of your wife: it is compulsory if you will ever amount to anything in ministry.

In the whole of scriptures, there are three or four kinds of marital callings. There is what I call the Sarah's/Abrahamic calling. When you know the kind of calling in your life in marriage, yours is to adjust to fit it (for lack of knowledge, my people perish).

In the Sarah/Abraham calling, there is an Abraham who from the foundation of the earth has been ordained to change the destiny of the world. And God must raise for that Abraham a Sarah that can play the role properly without becoming an obstruction in affecting the world. How does God do that? If you are married to a man with Abrahamic calling, you are in trouble. The man is not always very social. He shows his care, he shows his concern, yes but he doesn't bring flowers back. He doesn't have time for flowers.

I am teaching you this because there are too many books with western cultural background. European Christianity does not work in Africa and other parts of the world. All this wisdom of men, full of fantasies and imaginations, the romantic age is not realistic. I am now telling you the culture of scripture and that is our culture. I am not even talking about the culture of Africa because if you are talking about the culture of Africa or any human tradition you need deliverance in your marriage.

There are some of you who are landlords in your houses. It is not that you have any special calling, but since in Africa, the wife is a slave and she has to remain a slave, you treat her as one. It is not that she has chosen to call you Lord by kneeling down. You demand her to kneel down to serve you. That is the extreme case in Africa and it is unscriptural. When you are seated with visitors, the wife must not come close. It is an (abomination). She is not free at all. That is African tradition. If you are practicing that, the Lord will need to lift away the spirit from your life.

On the other hand, the western culture is another extreme that is not realistic. That is why they have more cases of divorce than we do. It is only the Biblical culture that is the answer, the power of God.

If you are married to an Abraham, he is a man of destiny. He is like Moses. He is so carried by the vision and the compassion of what God has called him to do. He is genuine, sincere and broken. I used to be so absorbed in the things of God that nobody thought I would ever get married. People thought that any woman I get married to had to die because I was so holy, so saintly, and too serious.

Most sisters would say, "How can you live in a house with a serious man like this? He is too serious! Every time, he either has a frown or a burden or a cry on his face. How can you live with him?" They wondered whether I was abnormal. And I am not too sure whether my wife has really gotten used to it now. You never get used to that kind of man. You just believe God that it is well. Because you can't understand his head and he cannot understand himself either. One time you are thinking this is his headache, he tells you the other one is the headache. When you are trying to put a balm, he says the headache has shifted to another place. You really wonder whether you can understand each other. That is the Abrahamic man.

He is the man that the Lord has used as an arrow to affect destinies and change the world and he pays the high price even if it means sacrificing his children. When you sacrifice your child, you have sacrificed your house, and you can sacrifice everything.

That is why Paul refused to marry. Paul became a eunuch by choice. It wasn't that God commanded Paul not to marry. Paul chose to remain unmarried because his life was a hard one. That was why he was the greatest of all the Apostles. Who would take the place of Paul? When you plan to go north, the Spirit tells you to go south. You can imagine what happens.

Peter belongs to the same category of Abraham. That is why Peter's wife is almost not mentioned in the Bible because he never carried her around. She couldn't keep pace with Peter. Something was burning in him. He is in this city – suddenly there is a vision that tells him to leave this city tonight. How many wives can cope? Some will give the man a query by tomorrow. They will murmur, quarrel and sometimes threaten divorce.

I was discussing with the wife of a deceased man of God sometime ago. They are very close to me as a family. He was my only close minister friend. His wife told me this, "Before, I would insist on going anywhere, walking side by side with my husband, so if he would take one step, I would take it with him. I wanted to travel with him everywhere because I felt that he was going too far. But I found out that he was like a crazy man. You can't program him. You follow him but he will be doing his things and forget you. I got tired of him and I told him, "Now you can go. You have my blessing."

The alternative she had was to file for divorce and go away. That is what the white man teaches us. If you are not compatible leave. She would have left. But who told her they were not compatible? Apostles, too, deserve to be married.

God made a provision because He knew for Him to breathe upon the earth and carry the earth along, there must be a man that breathes like Him and thinks like Him – and God neither sleeps nor slumbers. Such a man becomes as restless as God. So the wife must know how to adjust and fit that restlessness. Otherwise, she will sulk until she dies.

I know of another minister in Nigeria. This story shook me. It almost made me scared of marriage. The minister, though married, was moving and shaking his nation. The wife could not cope with the pace. She was also a woman of God. She was shaking her own small portion. But she always wanted to be with him everywhere he went. After much pressure, the man consented to their always traveling together. Still, she couldn't cope because she just couldn't understand the man. One day, she decided to pour kerosene on her body and set herself ablaze. The man returned home only to meet his wife on fire. What a tragedy! She is in heaven now. She didn't die immediately. She died after the third or fourth day. She wept for that one act. She cried until she went to heaven saying "God, I am sorry." She begged the husband to forgive her and said, "I am sorry I went too far this time around. Forgive me."

Some women are working themselves to suicide already, sulking and closing up. And yet some of them are very young. They still have many years to live but they have already withdrawn. Sickness and disease follow such people who go about with bitterness.

If your husband is the type that likes speaking in tongues, when he is in bed and won't allow you sleep when you are too tired, just leave the bed for him and find another place to rest. And then you can come back when the tongues are over.

I like what Rev. Ume Ukpai said in the Full Gospel National convention. He said there was a day God called him to pray in the night. He was burdened. He woke up to pray and he woke his wife and told her what God had said. The wife said he could go ahead and pray, she didn't hear God speak. She encouraged him to obey to God. Immediately, she turned her face to the other side and allowed him to pray. If it were another man, he would have concluded that he had married a demon, that the woman was against his faith. There are many men of God today who think their wives are demons.

That is why I don't compel my wife to do all the things that I do. That is why when there is an argument, I keep quiet and I go to obey what I must obey because when the sword comes, it will hang on me if I fail. It is me who will give account. It is my home on the line. Nobody will make me lose my head. That is why I tell people that if my wife cannot make me lose my head, no one else can. My wife is the closest person who can make me lose my head. If I can still keep my head in my house, then nobody can distract me.

You can imagine the man praying alone throughout the night and when the day of manifestation and blessings come, won't they share it together? I want to call on such men to mind their business. Don't try to force your wife or get your wife to begin to do five days of fasting with you when God spoke to you alone. There is no way she can feel the burden as you feel, as it was not laid on her as well by the Lord.

Stop fighting over things you shouldn't be fighting about. We want to be doing the same things together but it is not always possible. The day you got born again, God gave each one of you your responsibility. It may not necessarily be a big ministry but each one of you have a role with responsibility. It is a twofold ministry – one within the house for each other and the second one is outside the house for the Lord God Almighty. Every marriage has this dual ministry,

Any woman that is married to an Abraham must have a Sarah anointing. She must have Sarah's grace. She must be a woman who must be in charge at home, not the slave at home.

> *"Likewise, ye wives, be in subjection to your own husbands; that, if any obey not the word, they also may without the word be won by the conversation of the wives; While they behold your chaste conversation coupled with fear. Whose adorning let it not be that outward adorning of plaiting the hair, and of wearing of gold, or of putting on of apparel; But let it be the hidden man of the heart, in that which is not corruptible, even the ornament of a meek and quiet spirit, which is in the sight of God of great price. For after this manner in the old time the holy women also, who trusted in God, adorned themselves, being in subjection unto their own*

*husbands"* (1 Peter 3:1 – 5).

Some women think they cannot wear crowns for their house affairs. They are making a mistake. For the meals you cook in the kitchen, there is a crown of righteousness. Marriage is a ministry. For those of you who do not know, you had better take note. No matter how busy a woman of God is, she must still find time to cook for her husband very often and do those things that endeared her to him at the beginning of the marriage – this is how to honor him.

The Sarah woman takes charge of the house because Abraham has no time to attend to trivial or mundane matters in the house. When you see him at home, he is tired. He wants his meal. He wants to sleep. He wouldn't know how many people quarreled in his absence. That was why Abraham never knew how serious the quarrel between his wife and Hagar was. He never knew his wife was bitter. And even when he knew, he never knew how serious it was until the day she said, "My Lord, I have obeyed you over everything. But for this one, this woman is going." So the man went before God to complain that Sarah was beginning to break his regulations.

She was making life difficult for him by insisting that Hagar must leave. Perhaps he thought God would stamp his authority and say, "I am going to take her home so that you can marry a new wife, Hagar." But instead, God told him to hear the voice of his wife. God sided with Sarah meaning that since she remained where she belonged, her anointing was as important as the anointing of Abraham before God.

The woman is not doing an inferior job. That is where spiritual equality comes in. So, when we talk about sharing and partnership – that is where it come in. When everybody is playing his role, there won't be a problem.

Sarah would call Abraham, "My Lord." She was like the African traditional thing, "the cool and quiet wife," without becoming a slave. In the day when she would not take it any longer, she insisted that the circumstance change, and God sided with her anointing against her husband.

Moses married that kind of wife, in Zipporah, who added another dimension. Zipporah watched over the life of Moses so much that the day when death came, she saved him. In spite of all the anointing of Moses, he could not stop a small angel with one sword because he did not know what to do. He was always a busy man. He did not know when he was stepping on God. The woman carried him up and became a shield.

> *"And it came to pass by the way in the inn, that the Lord met him, and sought to kill him. Then Zipporah took a sharp stone, and cut off the foreskin of her son, and cast it at his feet, and said, Surely a bloody husband art thou to me. So he let him go: then she said, A bloody husband thou art, because of the circumcision."*
> (Exodus 4:24 – 26)

The woman with the Sarah anointing protects God's servant because the man once in a while becomes careless, and she will need to be there to raise the foreskin before the Lord to save his life. So, the woman has a ministry by herself. And that kind of a woman becomes a mother wherever she is. In the church, she teaches young women. She tells them how to operate. She takes charge at home in the same way she takes charge in the church. That is the woman with a Sarah calling.

There is the opposite of Sarah's which is Deborah's calling. In this case, it is the man that becomes a "woman wrapper." In the African words, when you are said to be a "woman wrapper," you had better get castrated because it is the greatest insult any man in Africa would take.

## DEBORAH ANOINTING

There is the Deborah's anointing where the woman God has called affects destiny and then it is the man that plays the complimentary role. Note that the Deborah anointing is one in a thousand mentioned in the scripture. There was a time of revival at the end of the 80's and early 90's, where every woman thought she was an Abraham. She had the anointing to change the whole world. Every woman just rose up and crowned herself Reverend (Mrs). Some are even called bishops.

The Deborah anointing is the other side of the Abrahamic anointing. You will notice that Deborah's husband was never mentioned. But did you hear of a divorce? We know that Deborah was married in the Bible. It is there that she was the wife of somebody. But the man was never mentioned as doing something spectacular. When men went to fight, he was there sitting at home because the wife had taken the place of a man to lead Israel. Without her, Israel wouldn't have survived. She was a woman of destiny.

Anybody with the Abraham calling is a man of destiny. He is destined to affect the destinies of many people and nations. Half of these who call themselves Apostles are not Apostles. They are just church Pastors. They should just bear titles like Pastor, Reverend and Bishop. The ordination comes by the oil of God that you carry. It doesn't come by the names and visions you saw. It is the practice that declares who you are, not the name. The name is just a positive confession that you want to be this thing but you are not yet.

I do not know why God chooses the men. Maybe because of the pressure that goes with it. The pressure in ministry needs a little bit of a balanced head to cope. It has taken a lot of balance in my head to keep intact with everything at once. Somebody asked me during one of the conferences, "Why don't you keep away for once? Why don't you let this thing go? You are coordinating this, you are coordinating that and still preaching in the pulpit. How do you cope?"

I told him it was not because I was the chief host or because we did not have enough facilities. If I did not give proper instructions, things will be messed up. We can only reduce the effect of pressure on people. We cannot stop it completely. Let us try to reduce it as much as we can but it takes somebody who has the grace of God inside to cope at that level.

There was this lady in Lagos, a Baptist lady, a wonderful singer, and of course a popular woman. Everywhere the woman went she pulled crowds. There was this time I met her in Kano during one of the programs I ministered at. The crowd was full and when she sang, people were carried up in glory. The Spirit of the Lord was everywhere. She left her husband at home to take care of their children. Her husband stayed more at home and she did more of the traveling. He would go to work, come back home and make sure that the children were doing fine. And he did it with joy.

Do you think that woman will carry a greater crown? If that man had not been what he was, the woman could not have succeeded. If you as the woman are not what you are, the man cannot succeed and then God will not be satisfied because God has not succeeded. Your success is God's success. Please identify your place and take it. Marriage is meant to be complementary. The crowns come from obedience.

In the midst of that high glory, the woman didn't know her husband planned to give her a pleasant surprise. He took a flight, arrived in Kano and drove in very late into the meeting. She had finished the last song and everybody was just screaming and worshiping the Lord. And just when she was going to hand over the microphone to the man who was leading, she turned and she saw her husband. Her heart fell and she was filled with rapturous joy.

Do you know what she did? Immediately, when she saw her husband, the woman handed over the microphone, ran and fell at his feet and said something like, "My Lord, welcome." She did not only hug him, she was hugging and holding his knees at the same time.

How many women could do that? She was the star before the congregation and yet when the real star appeared, she gave him his honor. That day, those who were more mature, those of us who could see in the spirit, saw the thing that was happening in the spirit. You can't destroy that woman because her life is an offering unto the Lord – a sweet smelling savor. No matter what creeps into her home, God will defend her.

I went to Ghana and I saw a family that touched my heart and I was impressed. The wife of one of the National Directors of the Full Gospel was a singer in Takuradi. When I saw the way the wife was behaving to her husband, I did not know she was important. But when she was invited to sing, I saw the same woman come out and take the microphone, and when she started, her voice was golden. She was not a liability to her husband. She was a gem.

There are people who have gifts but they refuse to manifest them. I have met so many men and women who used to sing very well but they don't sing anymore. What took away the song from their mouth? Marriage! There is war, they are depressed. They have become a shadow of themselves. If you have abandoned the gifts you used to have, it is time to awake from your slumber. You used to preach very well. Or you were an evangelist. Jesus can heal you today. Maybe as a woman in your youthful days when you were in the university, you used to lead – you were evangelism secretary. But today, you are only a kitchen evangelist. You only know how to cook food. God has to help you today. Whatever went wrong in your life the Lord will repair it. You used to have a prophetic calling but because of the many quarrels in the house, the prophetic gift has disappeared. Do you know quarrels cripple the anointing?

There was this minister, after he had finished preaching to a very large congregation, he would go back home and the wife would beat him like crayfish. He would be crying and say, "God have mercy on me." One day she would repent the next day she will go back to her demons. She did not stop it. And at the end, God took charge.

What happened to Nabal will happen to any man or woman who deliberately decides to becomes a torment or a hindrance to the other's oil (flow) and fulfillment in God's will, just because he or she is not satisfied with the other's portion and mannerism, or that the person has decided to stay outside God's will. Nabal was killed by God to loosen Abigail to marry a higher glory (David) because Nabal trampled on grace and would not allow God's flow (wealth) in him to serve God's will. 1 Samuel 25:37 – 38 says,

> *"But it came to pass in the morning, when the wine was gone out of Nabal, and his wife had told him these things, that his heart died within him, and he became as a stone. And it came to pass about ten days after, that the Lord smote Nabal, that he died."*

God will take you home or park you aside if you become the hindrance in your marriage to His will. Abigail did not initiate Nabal's death. God did. She never prayed for it. God realized the evil it would eventually do against His program and killed Nabal. It is God that decides whether to take your partner home or not, no matter his or her infirmity. Don't initiate it as God will record it against you and smite you for it.

If He leaves your partner alive, it means His workings are not over. Don't interfere. Otherwise, God will smite you in spite of your so-called righteousness. Abigail kept on playing her role completely in Nabal's life and the Lord's will. She never initiated God killing Nabal. Don't keep on doing righteousness looking up and waiting for the glory of the one who is to come, for whom you labor – Jesus Christ our salvation. He will clothe your nakedness with righteousness and keep you from falling.

Every minister must therefore, cultivate and woo his wife while he remains firm and in charge. The minister that loses charge, loses the direction of his ministry and calling. Let him guard her closely as one that guards the secret of his power. The wife that abuses these actions risks the danger of being smitten by God. No matter the attitude of the wife, the husband should guard her oils. It is his covenant in heaven.

# Personal Notes

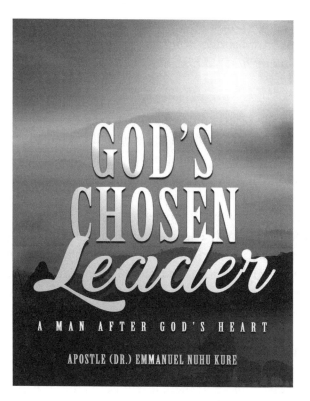

# CHAPTER 14

# Ministers, Be Warned!

I want the fear of the Lord to come upon us. God told me something in November 1997, that strange sicknesses will come upon the church. People who are supposed to find divine favor, people who have helped the church a lot because they were not careful to carry out their Christianity according to the heavenly order, will be affected.

*"For because ye did it not at the first, the Lord
our God made a breach upon us, for that we
sought him not after the due order."*
(1 Chronicles 15:13)

Although the priests did not know it, David the king knew it
and that is why God killed the man who dared to steady the
ark. And when they sought his face, he said it was because
they did not follow the pattern in heaven. God said, strange
plagues will come upon the lives of those who are going good
works, but are not following the pattern in heaven and are taking God for granted. They will be afflicted with strange sicknesses and diseases that no medical doctor can cure. God said,
some of them will be taken home. He will make them die so
that the church can mourn, so that the church can draw closer
to Him and find out "God, where have we gone wrong?"

More ministers will go home these years, ministers who think
they are life and death for people. Ministers who are boastful
in themselves, more of them are going home. It is part of the
program of God to sanitize the glorious church. Ministers who
have become too powerful in unrighteousness – they do unrighteousness and boast about it and will survive it. They survived other years, but they will not survive the coming years.

Some of you, God has saved your lives over many things.
But you will go back. You committed the first sin and God
saved you. You committed the second sin and God still saved
you. But God is warning that this time, if you commit a third
one, you will not come out of it. I am talking prophetically. If
you do not like prophecy, you are doomed because God uses
prophecy to bring out your nakedness. That is what the Bible
says prophecy is all about. Prophecy is not about how much
tongues you speak or how zealous you are. It is not a trick: the
more you see, the less you understand. Prophecy makes you

see Christ clearly as a mirror that changes you from glory to glory. That is how we know those who prophecy by the Lord and those who do not prophecy by the Lord.

Thank God for the churches in the cities in the south and in the north. Wherever the devil turns, God has a witness. God cannot be dead. There must be cities of refuge in all the churches and God is going to raise one in your church.

God asked me to tell the church that there is a particular sin she has been indulging in and taking it for granted – the sin of immorality. These days the church has taken that sin for granted and it might catch up with her. God made you a door of escape the last time because He was giving you a chance. If you go back again, you will catch AIDS. This is because you knew God's grace and took it for granted.

There is a mystery about God that is speaking. By the end of December 1996, God began to speak about taking ministers when He had given them a long time of grace. I have heard the fulfillment of two already, ministers who will do their rough play, and righteous play, and they still believe it is God's anointing.

There is a way ministers can be too proud. They will continue in iniquity and tell you that if you talk, you will die – especially Pentecostals. I think there is a need for revival among Pentecostal ministers. There is a need for healing because many of them are pente-rascals.

Unfortunately, judgment is coming up from the pulpit now. It is not from the congregation but judgment is coming from the pulpit. People are dying. To think of this makes me sober. One time I went on my knees and I said, "God, here am I, have mercy on me."

The Bible says,

> *"Who knoweth the power of thine anger? even*
> *according to thy fear, so is thy wrath. So teach*
> *us to number our days, that we may apply our*
> *hearts unto wisdom"* (Psalm 90:11 – 12).

God is healing those who are sincere. He is healing all those who remain righteous. But God is also resisting those who will dwell in iniquity, especially those who dwell in iniquity in the faith, who are deliberately and consciously taking his grace for granted. God is visiting them in judgment these days.

I see Jesus coming back. I see God forcing a revival through all the churches. I like one thing about the orthodox movement. There is a consistency in their structure that allows for their structure to continue to exist without being wiped out, so much that even in the days of backsliding, they still survive for the day of revival. So, the Lord always finds a church structure he can use.

The mystery about the Pentecostal churches is that when the president and founder dies, the church dies afterwards. That is not God's way of doing things. It is because three-quarters of the Pentecostal pastors build their church around them, not around the Lord Jesus and His gospel. If after my death, the ministry the Lord has helped me establish all over this nation dies, then I was not called of God. I was not called of God and the oil was not perfect. Ministry is supposed to continue to exist beyond the life of the pioneer leader. Wigglesworth is dead. But his ministry goes on. His books are alive and people's lives are being changed everyday because of that.

Ministers are going home. Strong men are going home. Great men are going home. Some of them will have to go home so that on the resurrection morning they can be there. I want to beg those who are pastors and ministers to search their lives just as king David cried and said,

> "Search me, O God, and know my heart: try me, and know my thoughts: And see if there be any wicked way in me, and lead me in the way everlasting" (Psalm 139:23 – 24).

## A CROWN TO WEAR

Are you still in the vision God gave you or you have left the vision behind? Are you now doing this work for the sake of your belly? Are you a man pleaser? If you look at yourself, what can you tell God you will receive a crown for? Can God say concerning you, "Thou faithful servant come unto my rest?" Is there any soul that you can look at and wear a crown for? Have you not read what Paul said, "You are our crowns in heaven?"

If at the end of life's journey you do not have a testimony in heaven, then you never lived a life. If at the end of a life's journey, whatever your profession and calling, you do not have a testimony, then you never lived on earth.

Those of you who know history are aware that at the end of every century, there is a shaking. Pastors who have been to Bible schools will tell you that every 2000 years historically, the world goes through a revolution. The first twenty years of this century, I have already said if rapture does not take place, we will be ushered into a space-age, even our cars will look like space cars. The CNN is already warning about that. In fact, CNN is showing future cars now and some of them you can climb over and cross over them because they are like a dish. They are round and very fanciful. Some of them are propelled by solar-light. They are so low that you five year old child might be taller than that car. The cars looks like space ships. Proto-types have been developed now.

The end is about to come. The battle is becoming more complex and sophisticated. It will take you every knowledge and understanding of the word of God to survive the times that are being confused now. It will take the kind of miracles or the testimonies we are hearing now for you to survive. And God is trying to equip us but we are running away from the presence of God.

We are remaining in our ignorance. The Bible says in the time of ignorance has God overlooked but now He commanded all men to repent. It is all men, not some men.

The period we are in now is a period of revolution. God has prepared a replacement to take over your seat if you prove unworthy, including Pastor Emmanuel Nuru Kure. There is another pastor who is prepared to take over my seat if I prove unworthy. If I become boastful, a vacancy will be declared and I will be on my way out.

The day Elijah said he was tired, a new person was chosen – Elisha – to take over. It was right there the Lord said, "You go back, anoint Elisha to take your place." If I am still alive and God tells me to anoint somebody in my place, that is unfortunate. May God not anoint somebody in your place.

The committee that will establish the anti-Christ is ready to take over the world. If you read the book of Revelation, fear will catch you. Our weather is very bad. There is a heated process. The world is getting warmer than before. Consequently, the weather is changing rapidly. It is not going to improve. It is going to get worse.

Let us leave our pride apart. I have stopped boasting as a pastor. Like I was telling somebody, I hardly know what happens in the town where I live. I drive from my house to the office and back doing what the Master has called me to do. I will not hear, let alone be disturbed by any gossips.

We have a crown to wear and there is a goal, but time is against us. We do not have time to quarrel. But if you want to quarrel, you are retired already. There is no space for you in the vineyard of God. There is no time for strife. If somebody is fighting over your chair with you, somebody wants to throw you out. The chair will be too hot for that person.

There is nothing to fight about. If you know your God, just relax. The period of strife has passed. The Bible says they that do know their God shall be strong and shall do exploits.

> *"And such as do wickedly against the covenant shall he corrupt by flatteries: but the people that do know their God shall be strong, and do exploits"* (Daniel 11:32).

Sometimes, I had to tell God to destroy the building in this ministry if He did not call me. If I stole, or killed somebody or took from somebody, something that was not to be taken, if I behave like other ministers who will tell you one thing and do the other, then Lord let this ministry waste." That was my prayer, and each time I prayed that prayer, the ministry increased. And I told God not to bring a ministry that eventually nobody will be able to control. He should give us enough that we can give account of in heaven. If you want to know the meaning of the kingdom, read the parables. That is where Jesus Christ kept on saying the kingdom of God is like this and that. Study the parables and compare them to the book of Revelation chapters 1 – 3 where it talks about the seven churches and the end time.

If you compare the two, you will understand the mystery of the kingdom of God and then you will ask yourself if you are pursuing the kingdom of God, if you are following the patterns of scripture or you are backsliding.

If you are a member that is fighting with his pastors, then you are not a Christian. If you are a member who is still fighting with you church, you are not a Christian yet. If you are still quarreling with your church about regulation or no regulation, you need to be born again.

There have to be regulations in the church to be able to guide the people. That should not be your business. Your business is, if Jesus comes now, are you ready to go home? Are you working out your salvation with fear and trembling? If your church does not do something, do not do it. If the church says do not speak in tongues, do not do it, at least not in the church because the church is somebody's property. But when you go to your bedroom and the Holy ghost comes upon you and releases you to worship the Lord the way you want, feel free to do so. If you find yourself shedding tears, please cry as you want. That environment belongs to the Holy Spirit. It does not belong to your church.

The Bible says in that day, God will not allow the destiny of the kingdom to be controlled by man.

> *"And in the days of these kings shall the God of heaven set up a kingdom, which shall never be destroyed: and the kingdom shall not be left to other people, but it shall break in pieces and consume all these kingdoms, and it shall stand for ever"* (Daniel 2:44).

That is, in that day He will raise His kingdom and He will

make His kingdom to be more powerful than all other kingdoms and the God of heaven will control them.

The Bible says we should not forsake the gathering of believers.

*"Not forsaking the assembling of ourselves together, as the manner of some is; but exhorting one another: and so much the more, as ye see the day approaching"* (Hebrews 10:25).

So, go to your churches, attend the programs, and obey according to the regulations of your church. Allow God to build your spirit in your church. There is a blessing in every church. There is no church, no matter how raw and inexperienced your pastor is that cannot be a source of blessing to you. The word of God renews itself. I want to correct this thing because many people are having misconceptions about many things.

Jesus is about to come back. But for those of you who do not know, the battle now is between the righteous and the wicked. And it has no church name attached to it. If you are a righteous man, the unrighteous will fight you. If you are an unrighteous man, the righteous will fight you. The righteous man shall not be apologetic to the unrighteous man because it is his business to offend Satan. The day I cease to offend Satan, then I have joined him. And it is Satan's business not to allow me breath. The day he allows me breath or ceases to attack, then we must be compromising somewhere.

It does not matter what church you come from. There are good and evil seeds. In very church, there are evil members, and in some cases evil pastors just as there are good ones. I told my staff in the ministry that I will not be surprised if there are Judas Iscariots among them because when the good seed was sown, an enemy came in the night and sowed an evil seed.

There are pastors that are in the occult. I do not know of any in southern Kaduna yet. But I know of many outside southern Kaduna. Some of these pastors who are in the occult still belong to some churches with big church names. There are also pastors who serve the Lord all their lives. And every day those two sets of pastors quarrel even in committee meetings.

There is no true church that is dead. I like what happened in the Methodist church some years ago. There was a little riot in the Methodist church and everyone that was an occult member was forced to take an oath that he was not in the occult. And many of them began to die from their oath. As far as I am concerned, that was revival. They should die if they will not repent or leave the church.

But why did that happen? Some youths who were called bloodsuckers had to block the road and insist that a particular corpse would not be buried until the cause of the death was unveiled. These youths were hitherto branded secret cult people because of their spiritual awakening. Anybody who sang and danced in the church was a blood sucker. But from that day, the truth was discovered and the real occult members began to die after the oath they had taken.

One of the things that led to the establishment of this ministry was the fact that when I first came to Southern Kaduna, I found church Secretaries and church Chairmen of orthodox and Pentecostal churches going to fulanis in the villages for medicine. I was an ordinary lecturer. If I advised them otherwise, they would tell me that they were elders in their churches and that it was even their pastors that referred them to the herbalist whom their pastors said were used by God. I wondered why

God would not use the pastors to heal the members.

And I got angry. There was a fire in my spirit. I said, "God, even if I am such a poor, dirty man, I beg you help me make a point in this land, so that we will not lose all our people to the herbalists. We will not have more demons in the church serving God. Make us a city of refuge."

And God is raising a standard in this ministry so that those who still do not want to do iniquity, who do not wat to go to herbalists can wait on the Lord. If they die, let them die. It is better to die in the Lord. It is better to know that you sought for a healing from God and He took you home.

## CAN GOD TRUST YOU?
I was addressing a gathering of leaders and ministers and I wanted to get the hand of God turned around. But it was proving difficult. I grappled with the Lord to get His hand to turn around to do a thing, but it was proving difficult and that confused me. I got a little bit restless. I did not know why His hand could not turn around like that.

I did not know the kind of people that were before me. I did not know the secret of their lives. I did not know their sincerity. I did not know they were the ones the Lord would want me to do that thing with because there are oils kept for particular people, and if you are trying to bend Him to give oil to those people that do not deserve it, He will not give them. He will hold back until the time comes. That is why He is God.

At a point, he started doing something: every scripture He had taught me on oil He would withdraw it or mix up the signals. I said, "God, why are you holding back? Why do you want to hide your face? Why will you not reveal yourself?"

I switched off and went into butter. Some of you do not know that butter holds the mystery of oil. God again switched off from the butter. I said, "God, do you have somebody in this congregation you hate whose face you detest to see? Or, are the majority of the people here not the ones you want to pour oil onto?

The Lord said He would be wasting His oil if He poured it on some of these ministers. He had not succeeded in getting their attention enough. The oil would make no meaning. Do not give good things to dogs lest they trample on it. They do not know the worth of it. I got disturbed. Rather, I heard God say, "The men I will choose, I will choose. The men I will release, I will release." God seemed to be talking about individuals, not a corporate release like that. They must be individuals. He will give corporate things to do, individuals by whom He will break grounds, that the prophecy must be fulfilled.

God said it is going to be like the Phinehas anointing. The Spirit of God will drop upon men. And when He drops upon men, He will give them an orientation of the Spirit. Their minds will be patterned to that orientation. These are the days of individual ministers' prophecy. Every minister has a appointed period of prophecy. If those days pass you by, your oil will become irrelevant. Do not let it pass you by. For many ministers, the hour is now but their voices have not begun to be heard because they are grappling with civilian affairs. You are busy settling family quarrels and house affairs. You are busy trying to settle one business deal or the other.

There are pastors that are businessmen more than they are pastors. I know of pastors who are so involved in business that they negotiate on behalf of their members. They are full time pastors. They are not part time. They want to dabble into every business deal of their members and make sure they have a share. I know of pastors who get members to be that front for them so that they can make money. They have an anointing. Instead of commercializing it directly, they use their members.

They say, "Look, I am going to get a business for you so that you can get a little income. I am helping you too. Bring the rest to me. It is my business. It is because I cannot remove the collar and go into business myself." You are either a consecrated full-time pastor or a full-time businessman. You cannot be both or part. God cannot use you. The oil cannot be split without repercussions.

When the Lord refuses to pour an oil, there are many reasons. There are leaders God cannot trust. If God cannot trust you, He will not submit Himself to you. There are people in the church God cannot trust enough to give the oil with which they can break new grounds. He will be wasting His time.

Can God trust you? Some of you are crooks. You will get the anointing and will use it to "make God see pepper" with it. You will spoil everything He ever bestowed in you. He knows you. He knows your pride. He knows what you are capable of doing. You will make human beings into slaves around you and treat them as property. You must settle these matters with God if you want Him to use you. His trust about your life is not perfect. Check your character and your habits. Check yourself in the mirror and let God begin to trust you again.

There are people who are not as restless about Him as He would have wanted them to be. How many of you, against your feelings, against your weakness, will still wake up early in the morning to pray? How many against the dryness around you will still struggle to read the Bible even if you cannot get any inspiration or edification? How many of you against the economic dryness and backdrop, against the political confusion, will take time to ask for God's will before you venture into a project? How many of you take advantage of every given opportunity without seeking God's perfect will? How many of you can say your zeal has not died yet?

When I cried to God to dip the people into the oil, He said, "My son, do you know what you are asking for? Do you know you are asking me to make them eat of the tree of life that they may live forever? Don't you know that in the day I dip them into the oil, some of them will die immediately? The oil, rather than keep them, will kill them because of their rudeness, hypocrisy, lying hearts and lying tongues. Their lips speak peace. But in their hearts, they are devouring spirits. Some of them have not been circumcised with the circumcision of fire. If I dip them into the oil, it will kill them because My Spirit is the Spirit of jealousy.

How many ministers are genuine? How many will want to serve God? The truth is that your habits, your character has refused to conform to God. Your emotions are not subject to the Holy Spirit. The seed must die first. Then it can it can resurrect. Where are the voices that can call down the new heaven and call forth a new earth?

**OIL SOAKED FEET**
Do you know that God can wash your feet with oil? Do you know that for Jesus to qualify to lift the gates of death, His feet had to be washed in oil? I repeat, for Jesu to qualify to lift away the whole foundation of hell, where Satan swells with all its fires, oils had to wash His feet. That woman brought the whole alabaster oil and held it, and all the blind Pharisees and blind religious people argued and said the woman was wasting this oil. She just ignored them and went ahead to wash His feet, not with water, but with oil.

The day God washes you with oil, there shall be a resurrection in the graveyards. He will change its foundations. Hell will be released the day your feet are washed with oil. Your problem right now is to get God to wash your feet with oil and your destiny will change. That is what I have been grappling with all these years. "God, here are my feet. I want to qualify." Joshua's feet were washed with oil. That is why he could say to the sun to stand still and it stood still.

Before you can come to the level where you can disorientate and manipulate and play with nature at will like the witnesses in Revelation 11, your feet must be washed with oil. The Bible says they had power to make rain fall at any time they wanted it to fall whether in the night or in the morning or in the afternoon. They also had the power to hold back the rain for as many years as they wanted. They did as they liked on earth. That is the loosening that comes when your feet are washed in oil.

The kind of power we need to change situations now is not an ordinary anointing falling. It is God again washing our feet. That is the key to changing the foundations of the dwelling of hell. I want ministers to learn this mystery. Notice when Jesus was to die, he was not anointed with oil. The woman with the alabaster oil did not pour it on His head. She washed His feet, symbolizing wherever the soles of His feet would step upon, He would take.

She washed His feet. She did not anoint His head. Do you know why? The head is the doorway to power. The feet are the doorway to possession. The head is the doorway to power where power is controlled in your life. But the feet are the release door to possession. By this anointing, Jesus was released to take hell and to change its place. There is the washing of the feet and there is the anointing of the head.

It was when the oil washed Jesus' feet that people in the room began to protest. They did not know that it was the spiritual mystery that had released the anointing to open up and take over that which was impossible, that which closed up for eternity; that which only God had the key to the dwelling of hell. That was the mystery. The woman did a foolish thing by human standards. But it brought out a resurrection. That is why, in the day when all men fled from Him at the cross, the oil kept Him. The Father kept His covenant.

A day will come in your life when you will be the only one defending the righteousness of your life, the calling on your head when you will be the only one standing alone, not even your family members will be there. Even if they wanted to help, they will be helpless. It will take the secret oil that you have to keep you alive.

> *"At my first answer no man stood with me, but all men forsook me: I pray God that it may not be laid to their charge"* (2 Timothy 4:16).

That was Paul reporting before kings and he was telling Timothy what had happened to him. He had never seen that humiliation in his life before. He said in the days of his trouble, in the day of the challenge of his oil, all men forsook him.

Friends, we are in the day when people will shy away from the truth. People will not be bold to hold on to the truth. Very few will stand by the truth especially were the truth is bringing trouble. They will distance themselves.

We are coming to a time when righteousness will have to defend itself. You will need the washing of your feet with oil to give you the stamina you need to speak back. It is the washing of your feet that brings the fitness that speaks for you in the days of impossibilities.

The spiritual washing of feet is not by water. I am not preaching the doctrine of your church on washing your feet with water. I am not in agreement with that. I am talking about a deeper mystery, that which the finger of God does. Paul said at the first hearing, no one stood with him. All men disappeared. All men forsook him. I like the King James Version. It used the word "forsook."

Can you imagine Paul, the most popular evangelist of his time could one day stand alone in a battle? He was someone people were proud to relate with – people were proud to be associated with him. Some would say, "I am the friend of Paul." But there was a day when Paul stood and he stood alone. And all men forsook him including the brethren. So, will it be surprising to you if by tomorrow you are forsaken by all including your closest associates?

Every minister has to go through this once in his life – a day when only you and your oil and your sincerity will be standing. Every other thing will disappear. Get ready for that day. If you do not have stamina, you will fall on that day. That is what I faced in 1997. For the first time, I had to go back to the sincerity of my oil, the roots of my calling. It was the only thing that convinced me to keep on going and not that I had encouragement anywhere.

Everywhere I entered was a broken reed. I was smitten, and I knew without God, I could not bear this alone. I had to tell God I could not carry it alone. If it went further, I would die by myself. I would collapse by myself. I would stop this preaching by myself. I asked God to take away this cup from me. I had never felt myself in the pit of hell like I did then and I was forced to do many stupid ridiculous things. I call them stupid now, and any time I remember, I tell God to forgive me. I did not know I could still be childish. Fear can make many things happen. I only knew my struggle. Only the oil stood by me.

That was the mystery Jesus went through. The oil stood by him on the cross. The oil became the witness when all men forsook him. That was the level at which the son of man was left alone. Now here is the most popular evangelist of his generation, Paul saying that he was lonely for one day. It is like me telling you I was lonely sometimes then, and you may wonder if I can be lonely in Nigeria. You do not know the mystery of God in this gospel. The day comes when only you can stand alone.

The closest of people can deny you, not because you have sinned, but because the righteousness you are manifesting is so hot that they fear it will bring them into trouble. So, they keep off. These are the kind of days we are entering into now, days when unless you manifest that kind of fierce anointing, the situation will not change. You must be ready to manifest that fierce sincerity, fierce righteousness, bold faith speaking. If you cannot operate faith so boldly and violently and drastically, some situations cannot be corrected. There are times you need to take some drastic steps, drastic decisions that could save situations. Otherwise, the situations will not change.

That is what I was praying in 1997 especially in one of the South-Western zones where we had a crisis, one that God would not lay upon the brethren and they were not bold on the day of truth. I was looking for witnesses who would help, who were there and saw what happened. Only one or two people spoke out at that time. Only one or two spoke out the realities.

Others, who were strong men, elderly men whom we thought could speak and silence the others kept silent. They sat on the fence. My head was scattered because of what I was seeing all around. I did not believe the church could come to that level of pettiness. They were not bold. They did not commit unrighteousness thought. But they also did not see nor come out to defend righteousness. I saw a clear manifestation of the end times.

God remembers that for those who do that, He cannot trust them tomorrow. That is why Paul had to pray for them and say, "May God forgive them." God will forgive. You will go to heaven. But when God wants to do a drastic thing, He will not trust you. He knows you are capable of forsaking Him a second time. May that not happen to you in Jesus' name.

The days ahead are going to prove you. Will you forsake Him? Will you play the role of a linesman? The days ahead are going to test your anointing. To hear the truth might bring you reproach. Will you stand or will you forsake Him? The Peter's test is coming again. The test of the disciples at the death of Jesus is coming again, Will you forsake Him?

God wants children to establish His kingdom on earth. If there are childlike men, they will establish the kingdom. These sophisticated Christians who know scripture from Genesis to Revelation – these are men who know how to manipulate in wisdom and obedience. No matter which way the coin is tossed, they never lose. They always know how to find ways of escape in everything. God will not trust a Christian with that character because something is wrong. That is not perfect submission.

It takes a perfect submission and a vision of Him, a vision of His mercy for you not to be able to deny Him in the day of the greatest test of your life. Then you can have a story, then you can have a testimony to tell. Then you can say you fought with dragons and you destroyed them. Paul said he fought with animals, that he fought with dragons. How many of you will say so.

I have seen a little bit of that. I do not know how that one will manifest again in my future. But thank God I have had a taste of that, how it feels like. I preached it, but now I have tasted it, that the best of people you respected with the whole of your heart will do righteousness by diplomacy. They do not know they are hurting the heart of the Christ they love so much by their diplomacy, which does not bring out truth clearly. But they avoid and tell you to forget it and not to quarrel with deceit. If you do not quarrel with deceit, it will kill you. It will destroy the church. Somebody has to do something to stop it. If you want to do it softly as others will say, the kingdom will suffer some set back. "Do it softly" is the language the devil likes to hear. "Do it softly" and before you open your eyes, he has finished with you.

## MINISTER'S TIME
When a minister is not praying or resting or fulfilling a secular responsibility, he must occupy his time fully, doing either of the following:
- Reading
- Exhorting (Sharing Christ or encouraging others)
- Searching Biblical doctrines – understanding Jesus and what His teachings are actually all about

This will not only destroy idleness and any avenue that Satan uses to break the hedge, but establish a continuous altar of fellowship between the Holy Spirit and His servant.

This is also the secret behind developing and releasing the gifts that are in you. It is the power derived from these three activities of obedience that gives the gifts in you the PUSH to manifest and keep you alive and active in the spirit.

That is why Paul told Timothy,

> *"Till I come, give attendance to reading, to exhortation, to doctrine... Meditate upon these things; give thyself wholly to them; that thy profiting may appear to all. Take heed unto thyself, and unto the doctrine; continue in them: for in doing this thou shalt both save thyself, and them that hear thee."* (1 Timothy 4:13 – 16).

# Personal Notes

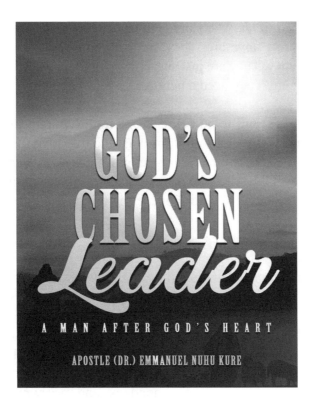

# CHAPTER 15

## The Plight Of The Church

We have come to the place of birth as a church but the strength is not there. It's been proving difficult to give birth. There is a generation of men that will take over the battle. Men the Lord has kept and ordained to take the place.

I have noticed in the last three years that the missionaries in the mission fields are getting discouraged. Many are getting out of their fields. Many are getting sick and many are not doing anything anymore. They are just going round and round in stagnancy. They are just surviving. For many, their enthusiasm is gone. They need a new zeal, a new baptism.

Something seems to be going wrong in the church. Go to the cities and you will also find out that the true love for God is dying. There is an increase in religious activities because of insecurity. Only a few believers are interested in sitting down to hear the word of God. For the majority, all they want are miracles.

I am saying this because by signs and wonders, God has changed almost a generation through my humble self. I have found out that I struggle to tell people about Jesus. But they hear me because they know a miracle will come after, not because they really want to know about Jesus. They take it for granted that they already know him. He came to die that they might be healed, that is just the summary of it – that they might receive a miracle, that goodness and mercy might follow them.

Their lives are not recreated and transformed and each time I do this, I feel pain inside and cry, "Lord, where is the generation that loves you? Where are the people whose heart is toward you totally? Where are the men that will be raptured? Most of the people who receive miracles now are not going to be in heaven. Jesus said it himself that they came because of the bread and butter, not because they loved him.

> *"Jesus answered them and said, Verily, verily, I say unto you, Ye seek me, not because ye saw the miracles, but because ye did eat of the loaves, and were filled. Labour not for the meat which perisheth, but for that meat which en-*

*dureth unto everlasting life, which the Son of man shall give unto you: for him hath God the Father sealed"* (John 6:26 – 27).

He had only a few disciples. Even among the disciples, there were those with mixed oils. I fear the prophecy of the Lord Jesus spoke Himself that, "As it was in the days of Noah, so shall it be in the coming of the Son of man," is going to be fulfilled in our generation.

God told me that if the rapture had taken place in the days of Noah, only one person would have entered heaven. Eight people were saved from the flood, but only one would have entered heaven. This is because he was the only one who believed God. The others got into the ark out of respect for their father. When Jesus said, "As it was in the days of Noah," He was speaking with a foresight that even the eight will not be found. It will be the equivalent of one. If only the equivalent of one percent of the present generation of the church that will go to heaven, something is really wrong.

How many will go from Nigeria? How many will go from your country? Will you be among them? How are you sure you will be there? I really get disturbed by this and if there is anything that is trying to discourage me in ministry, it is this reality. After laboring over a thousand souls, I ask myself is it really worth it? Where is the one that has really turned around? Am I part of the generation that is maintaining the status quo or a generation that is moving the kingdom forward?

God said, the church either breaks through now or the dark age will take over. We have come to the verge of giving birth. The nations have come to the verge of explosion, violence (physical and spiritual), plunder and wasting. The UN is at its verge, the whole of Asia is at its verge, they are all restless now. Prophecies are being fulfilled so rapidly that men's hearts in our generation will begin to fail them. We have come to that verge and the church seems to be pouring oil that is not making an impact. So, we have found ourselves in a very desperate position. The Lord told me some years back that soon, if there is no bursting forth from the church, there shall be a dark age when everything that exists will be used as a destructive instrument. One day, animals will almost talk like men because of the cloning that is going on in science. We are at the verge of either a dark age or the rapture. Remember what Ecclesiastes says that everything that is now, has been before, nothing is new on the earth. This means we are all going round and round.

The Spirit of God tells me if the trumpet does not sound now because of the church, the dark age will set in and take over. The ministers are no longer ministering because they rarely care for the life of the sheep. Today, God is going to call men that are ready to die. Men, who are coming in, not because of what they are going to get from it, but men ready to die for the Lord.

I have faced death so many times that earthly goods have lost their meaning to my life. Unless the Lord gives you power to keep them, they shall be travail for your soul. You will have them but you cannot sleep.

**THERE IS HOPE FOR THE CHURCH**
The Lord spoke the following mysteries to me concerning the church. He said, **"there is coming the major move of the Holy Spirit in the waves. A mighty wind, mighty power will sweep over the nations. Great waves will move the countries and great revelations as has never been seen for a long time will manifest. Revelations that will show us the way and guide nations; things that will happen many**

years ahead shall be shown in that day. Men will know the program and the calendar of the Most High. In that day, they shall eat the bread of angels. They shall live by the Spirit of Him that called them. Great men of revelation will be born. Men who will call forth a generation; men of the Spirit.

The earth shall stand still before them. It shall quake before their feet. Men who by strange manifestations shall call forth a resurrection of dead bones that were already accounted for death. They shall rule and bring down waves of my Spirit and power from heaven. They shall give birth to a generation. It shall come to pass that by strange miracles shall their life styles exist. They shall not stay in one place but shall move as the wind moves them, they and their households. They shall move as the nomads in the days of their prophecy. And wherever they prophecy, life shall come forth. Men shall be born and nations shall come forward. In that day, the fear of them shall be upon the nations and the dread of them shall cover the earth. Their death shall be by me, just as their lives were by me.

I shall own everything. I shall move them like a tent and the glory shall cover wherever they enter. Call forth men unto me. Let there be a retreat, a withdrawal unto my dwellings for the wrappings of my glory to come that I may ordain them and release them that the last oils for the nations might go forth," says the Spirit of the Lord.

Strange men they are, strange men they will be. A new specie of saints is about to be born – men that have the keys of the nations – men whose zeal shall not die according to the pattern of spiritual death that is coming over the church now.

Beyond the revival we think we are having now is a level of

death that is coming upon the church. We only try to keep a front that we are alive. But in reality, there is death coming over the church. Living dead Christians are walking. If not for God keeping His testimony, our nakedness would have been on the street. Do not be carried away by the clothing you see outside. There is a deadness inside.

We have come to the point when something has to break loose in our nation and in the nations. Otherwise, a dark age will come. Unto whom the arm of the Lord revealed this day? Unto whom is the Lord stirring a matter? Upon whom is the burden of destiny resting that the Spirit of the Lord might lift him out of his seat so that a generation might receive life by his obedience?

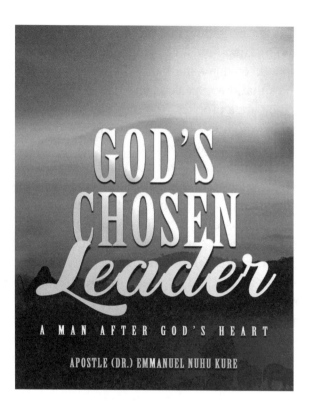

# CHAPTER 16

## The Phinehas Anointing

Where is the Phinehas that will establish God's glory by the violence of his javelin? Where is the man that dare carry the javelin anointing? Where is he that will become the firebrand of the nations, the conscience of the nations? Where is the man that will carry the prophetic and yet an evangelistic anointing that will break fresh grounds?

These days we are getting into prophetic evangelism. If you are going into mission fields, get prophetic unction along with it. It is prophetic evangelism that will change situations. Prophecy to the situations. Speak as an Oracle. When you speak as a oracle, you are a prophet. You only say that which you hear, and see that which is a burning. You do not speak from your heart. Where is the man that God's hand is coming upon? Let him arise. Let us go ad break the nations together. Let us go and establish a fresh oil. I have a burden that there is so much carelessness, nonchalance about the tide, the way the church is flowing. Everybody is thinking about himself or thinking of himself. The people of our generation including the church are rebellious. Men are being born but they are scavengers who want to plunder the Lord who died for them. They want to get his anointing and yet not serve his purpose.

Pray and ask God that you do not want to be counted among the dead in our generation. Let God loosen you from among the dead. There has to be a breakthrough. Let God tear away the wall of partition in your life.

"I must see Jesus!," should be your cry. This matter is beyond just reading and being comfortable with the word. You must see Jesus. Your heart must begin to get disturbed about a matter. Hear what God said through Isaiah,

> *"Thus saith the Lord, As the new wine is found in the cluster, and one saith, Destroy it not; for a blessing is in it: so will I do for my servants' sakes, that I may not destroy them all. And I will bring forth a seed out of Jacob, and out of Judah an inheritor of my mountains: and mine elect shall inherit it, and my servants shall dwell there. And Sharon shall be a fold of flocks, and the valley of Achor a place for the herds to lie down in, for my people that have sought me"*

The Lord said what our spirit should begin to cry for is the new wine in the cluster. We must discover the new wine. We must break protocol. We must enter into a desperate situation. We have tried. We want to try but the situation is not healed. Then it is time to go beyond the ordinary boundary of the natural. It is time to seek the Lord.

God is looking for men who will not follow him just because they want security. They must be men who really want to know His personality, men who really want to get introduced in their spirit to the real Person, men who dare call Him, "My father and God, do with me as it pleases thee."

When you truly find God, your heart will not be satisfied. There shall be a restlessness that seeks for more. There shall be a peace within you but there shall also be a restlessness that desires more of God. There is new wine hidden somewhere and somebody has to find it to save our generation. The new wine makes the difference. But the men that have it are not many. Somebody needs to find the secret place of God and save our generation now. There is a vacancy in the air for people who will change the phase and the pace of evangelism and missions who will begin to satisfy the cry of God.

## YOU MUST DENY YOURSELF
Jesus said that if a man will come after him, he must first deny himself, take up his cross, he must die first to self, and then follow Him.

> *"Then said Jesus unto his disciples, If any man will come after me, let him deny himself, and take up his cross, and follow me. For whosoever will save his life shall lose it: and whosoever will lose*

The Phinehas Anointing                                    167

*his life for my sake shall find it."*
(Matthew 16:24 – 25)

We do not have so many of such people any more in ministry. They are not dead to themselves, neither are they carrying the cross. They are very much alive. You must begin to repent and die to self. God must find the quality of men He used to find in the Bible in you. The prophet Jeremiah was not afraid to die, yet did he die? No! He was brought close to death many times by violent men but was never slaughtered by a violent man. Paul was not afraid and in his generation there was no man like him yet. Men tried to make nonsense of his existence, yet in his last three years, he had a good accommodation to himself. What about Peter who shook nations and dined with kings and yet learned how to speak with poor men in the gutters so that the kingdom might be established? Yet in the day of their death, they did not hold back their lives.

Lay down your life and you shall find it. David lived beyond the generation of kings who declared him dead. Isaiah the prophet never died by a violent man. Where are men who even in death shall speak? Today, we have shortlisted men who served God? They lived for themselves, no thought of leaving a generation behind. Their condemnation is already settled in heaven.

We must let go of our lust, ambition, programs, etc. If God called you to the field, you must totally give in. If you feel tired in the field, come out for a while to be refreshed by the Lord before going back. That way you can renew your oils for effective and efficient labor.

## TO PROCLAIM RESURRECTION, YOU MUST DIE!
I have said this before, the Spirit strongly make me say it again, that there are three paramount central things that if a

minister does not serve in his life, he needs not go into ministry. First, he must die, die to self and to his will. Jesus said,

> *"Then said Jesus unto his disciples, If any man will come after me, let him deny himself, and take up his cross, and follow me. For whosoever will save his life shall lose it: and whosoever will lose his life for my sake shall find it."*
> (Matthew 16:24 – 25)

You take up your cross to hang yourself on it. In the days of Jesus, the criminal carried the cross he was hung on. Until you hang yourself, your will, your desires, your secret sins, until you are willing to be everything He desires you to be without fine-tuning it, you will end up working for yourself, not for Him. If you cannot hang yourself on the cross you carry and leave Him an empty shell to put into it whatever he wills, then you are not ready to be used.

You must be willing to forsake everything. You must forsake building a future for yourself in this world. You must have had Him inside of you as your personal Savior and Lord and be enjoying sweet fellowship with Him. Personal friends and public image must be decided by Him and not become a personal drive.

You must not be ruled by the normal flow of human demand and responsibility that is placed on you daily but choose and do what is his will, second by second. Luke 9:59 – 62 says,

> *"And he said unto another, Follow me. But he said, Lord, suffer me first to go and bury my father. Jesus said unto him, Let the dead bury their dead: but go thou and preach the kingdom of God. And another also said, Lord, I will fol-*

*low thee; but let me first go bid them farewell, which are at home at my house. And Jesus said unto him, No man, having put his hand to the plough, and looking back, is fit for the kingdom of God."*

The very day you look back and regret leaving all to serve Him, that day you have failed and disqualified yourself. Let our love, hunger and devotion to Christ be such that it cannot be shared with anyone or anything else. This is the spirit that conforms us into His image.

*"I am crucified with Christ: nevertheless I live; yet not I, but Christ liveth in me: and the life which I now live in the flesh I live by the faith of the Son of God, who loved me, and gave himself for me"* (Galatians 2:20).

Except we become disciples first and tutored by the Holy Spirit, we cannot replicate Christ in any situation. "Remember Lot's wife," lest you become a pillar of salt halfway into your calling.

You must stop seeking for an easier way to the kingdom, you must go through the cross to be worthy. You must be crucified that He may come alive through you. You must die before you can proclaim the resurrection. There can be no fellowship between God's Spirit and you except there is a broken crucified life.

Having gotten all these, get a forgiving spirit. A forgiving spirit will set you loose and break all strings. No mystery or spell can hold you bound with a spirit that forgives freely and holds nothing to heart except CHRIST.

## A GENERATION HAS TO BE BORN

My brethren, a generation has to be born. Nigeria and the world at large are looking for it. You must look for the new wine. A seed must be brought out of Jacob, and out of Judah, an inheritor of my mountains.

I fear that if the present generation of priests passes away, there will be no people to fill their vacancies. To make things worse, the present generation of priests will not allow inheritors to take over. They fear competition and so, keep those who should take over afar. So, even by design, the devil is crippling the church. The voices are not being allowed to speak. Rather people are learning the wrong patterns, becoming selfish. God never lived without an inheritor, a witness, a Joshua.

God is ready to break the walls and release men who will go like fire. You are not only meant to pray, but also to pull down. Bring down by physical contact and confrontations against the kingdom of darkness. Arise and go! Stand over the city and prophesy and let a generation in that city be born for God. God is looking for "mad men" who do not look at the winds and faces. He told Jeremiah, "You shall not look at their eyes and faces." Do not get involved in civilian affairs. Mind the business of the One Who sent you.

> *"Be not afraid of their faces: for I am with thee to deliver thee, saith the Lord. Then the Lord put forth his hand, and touched my mouth. And the Lord said unto me, Behold, I have put my words in thy mouth. See, I have this day set thee over the nations and over the kingdoms, to root out, and to pull down, and to destroy, and to throw down, to build, and to plant"* (Jeremiah 1:8 – 10).

Do not mind the anointing of others and their mode of operation. It is not your business. Your business is to mind your own anointing.

God is giving birth to a generation of peculiar anointings and revelations. They will not get into mysticism. But by strange operation of faith, they will change their generation. An anointing is coming. But those who will carry it are those who are ready to go the next mile with God – those who want to partake in rapture. The rapture anointing is the anointing by fire and its working is a devouring work. It devours and eats up. It is the violent that rule now and it will take a greater violence to control them. So, only "mad men" can answer the present madness in our society. Your anointing must be stirred to the level whereby you become like a mad man on a suicide mission.

You had better know that what is happening in the Arab world (the suicide bombers) is like a prophetic thing. They put themselves with fire, go and explode and die with it. That is like a prophetic action. It will take that kind of violence to control and survive the times except that the Arabs are championing a negative sanity. Even in the spiritual, it will take a devouring fire to bring sanity. Many peoples' hearts no longer want to seek the Lord and it will take a groaning and a devouring fire to draw their attention.

People admire my calling, but I am not satisfied with myself. I fear we are losing the battle and I fear it is my fault. Why should I fear it is my fault? Yet that is the feeling I cannot suppress. I feel and believe that if I have not failed, my country cannot fail. If I succeed, then Nigeria should succeed. Let it be said that it is because of people like you, a remnant is being left in Nigeria – that some sanity is still being kept and some control still exercised.

In Revelation chapter four, there is what is called the seven Spirits of God.

And He that sat was to look upon like jasper and a sardine stone. And there was a rainbow round about the throne, in sight like unto an emerald. And round about the throne were four and twenty seats. And upon the seats were four and twenty elders sitting, clothed in white raiment. And they had on their heads crowns of gold. And out of the thrones proceeded lightening, and thundering and voices. And there were seven Spirits of God. And before the throne there was a sea of glass like unto crystal. And in the midst of the throne were four beasts full of eyes before and behind.

The seven Spirits walk to and fro on the earth. And the time will come when the dwelling of those seven Spirits will be on earth. The Bible says those seven Spirits are seven burning flames of fire. So, imagine them going through the earth burning everything in their way. The anointing that will manifest on earth will come in seven flames. Have you forgotten that the power that released the early church came as tongues of fire? That power brought down the glory of God. But now that power will be devouring the thing that comes against the church. That is why in Isaiah 29:6 the Bible says by the flame of a devouring fire shall the Lord visit his people.

Moses also had a strange manifestation of fire. It was fire that called him into service. You must begin to ask God to lift away the old garment. Ask for new anointing and new wine – the one that speaks by fire. The Bible says that Jesus shall baptize you with the Holy Ghost and fire. Why is there the Holy Ghost before the fire? Because the conclusion of the matter in our generation shall be by fire. God shall now begin to speak by devouring, and when He devours, a remnant shall not be found. That anointing must burst forth now. Otherwise, there shall not be hope.

Where are the men today who are ready to take the anointing that will save our generation? Where are the men that burn and carry the flames? You must seek for it. Let God find you and release you. Who will go to the field? Who wants to change the destiny of this world?

**THUS SAYETH THE LORD**
This revelation and prophecy came to me on a pulpit in a major gathering of saints in Asaba, Nigeria. "I see a tumbling, a tumbling and a tumbling, and nations shall tumble. In the coming dispensation shall be the trembling of many nations. It shall come to pass in the day of their tumblings a fire shall burst forth. It shall be the kindling of my Spirit and in that fire, all that will speak guile shall be consumed. All that shall stand against my will, I shall cast coals upon them. By the coals, a generation shall be wiped out and there shall be wars, great and strange wars where there are no victors.

In the midst of those wars, a great harvest shall take place and it shall be accounted for the multitude. In the midst of these wars, the nations in the midst of blackness shall know glory. They shall be filled with glory and my fear shall be upon the nations and upon the earth. Then will I send the deliverer, and your redemption shall come speedily, saith the Spirit of the Lord."

"Arise, wash your feet. Arise, put on your linen. Put on sandals for behold my mantle is in your hands. I put it in your hands. Go forth and take the grounds and grounds shall stand before you. Arise, for in you is kindling of fire and the fire shall burn. I see men, a great force stripped naked with nothing pulling them down. I see them released as men of war. I see them walk as ancient warriors with great spears in their hands. And in that day, their voices will stop the heavens. Their voices will open the earth. In that day, there shall be great earthquakes. They shall become a mystery for life and death will be in their tongue. In their days, men will say, 'the Lord reigns.'

"Arise, for the consumption is gone before you and your strength is restored. He that lifts up his eyes shall receive a flame. He that has stepped out in obedience shall burn in the fulness of My power. And I shall manifest you by a strange revelation. And in that day you shall not have your own heart. I shall take away your heart from you and shall put My heart inside of you. You shall not think or talk like men but shall think and talk like I would.

Then men would fear for they would say, 'God is come down amongst us. Who shall abide? Who shall stand?' Arise, Arise, for my chosen, my elect are here and My finger is come upon them. I have loved you with an eternal love. I would hide you in the secret place. None shall know the secret of your dwelling. Men shall be bewildered at you because of my manifestation. Go forth, for a history shall be written again and a generation shall remember you. Go forth, for there shall be great minds abroad. Go forth, for My Spirit will stir the matter up around. The nations shall know it for the stirring shall be great."

**BY FASTING SHALL FIRE COME**
The Spirit says you should come before God and take a fire in His presence as individuals. He says by a fast, you shall separate yourself. There are some the Lord will put on their heads to separate themselves by a forty-day fast. There you will take the fires. During the fast, there shall be a loosening of everything and there shall be a clothing. There shall be a release of all the ornaments that you need.

You shall catch fire there. During the forty-day fast, there shall be experimentation in heaven for the Lord shall court your spirit. He shall woo your spirit. He shall descend and break the veil. He shall speak to you as person to person. He shall begin to give you instructions and He shall make you find confirmation in the word concerning some of the instructions. It shall come to pass that as He lays His hands, and impresses things and writes inside the tablet of your soul, you will begin to obey some of them even during the fast.

In those passages, He will give you direction on what to do next. He says for some at the end of this fast and while the fast is yet going on, signs and wonders will begin going on. At the end of the fast, you shall make your obedience complete by breaking off unto the field of your calling. He said for some there shall be a turning that shall continue for six months after the fast. After six months, there shall be a release of rivers that no one can stand.

In that day, I shall translate the literal word into fire in your soul. For the word that you hold in your hand, even the Bible, shall become fire in your home, and the deep mysteries from it shall speak. The person you were six months before shall not be the person that you will become six months after. For the revelation of the word shall be mighty. In the day when you speak, rivers will fall, deliverances will come. And he shall send you to fields and you shall put the fields on fire and the fire shall burn the fields.

Some of you will become like traveling evangelists into the fields and shall stay there for months to work with the missionaries that are stationed there. And the ground shall break. In the day the ground breaks, you shall not start anything there but will leave it unto the missionaries. Then leave the field for another field. You shall travel round in a missionary journey breaking grounds and yokes. Ye shall not ask for sandals or garments for He shall feed you. You shall not beg for money, for He shall provide your needs. He said for a year shall some of you go round nations and wherever you stay, His glory will break the grounds.

I see men in the church that are called waters. You shall bring forth not only inspiration but shall restore hope in the field. I see a pattern that is ordained only by heaven. You shall go back and take the fires. By fasting shall the fires come. For some, it is ordained unto forty days. Ye shall take the challenge. For the Lord God has waited for this day. I see Him standing upon His altar and the whole of the heavens is quiet. Even the trumpeters are quiet and I see their eyes set upon those grounds. For there is a solemnity on earth because of this great thing that is about to happen.

For the day for the wiping of the tears and groaning of the heaven is come. For the day of His power is come. There shall be an earthquake and the shaking shall start in your bones. In that day, there shall be restlessness, and your spirit will not mind until the oil that it carries is released. This is what I see from on high. You shall go back to Him and He shall fill you with what you do not have. And you shall receive of His word. For in the day that the word does not speak, the Spirit of the Lord shall resist you by Himself.

> *"For I testify unto every man that heareth the words of the prophecy of this book, If any man shall add unto these things, God shall add unto him the plagues that are written in this book: And if any man shall take away from the words of the book of this prophecy, God shall take away his part out of the book of life, and out of the holy city, and from the things which are written in this book."*

(Revelation 22:18 – 19)

I hear Him say that He shall protect the integrity of His word. Yea, there shall be no manipulations. Her that manipulates the word shall be smitten.

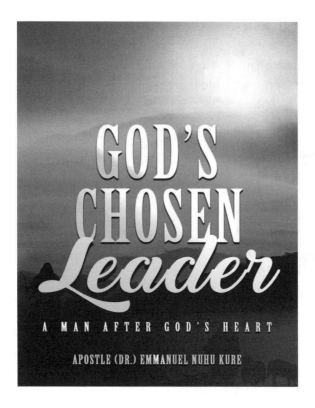

## Postlude

If this book has been a blessing to you, we would like to hear from you. In addition, if you need to contact the author, please write,

Apostle Emmanuel Kure
Throneroom Trust Ministry
P.O. Box 266,
Kafanchan, Kanduna State,
Nigeria
Telephone: +234-812-2736-711
+234- 805-6442-754
Email:ttmvisionpioneeroffice@gmail.com

## OTHER BOOKS

We invite you to log on to Amazon.com for the following books that are available there:

Practical Prophetic Prayer and Warfare is an imperative strategy to equip the Church with a critical spiritual arsenal, enabling her to contend with and defeat wickedness in heavenly places. Dr. Kure outlines many vivid and lucid fundamentals of satanic warfare, equipping Christians with the necessary weapons to be continually victorious in their battle with the kingdom of darkness.

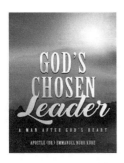

Written by a seasoned Christian warrior on the front lines of spiritual warfare and satanic witchcraft in Nigeria, Africa, God's Chosen Leader is meat for believers equipping them with proven, pragmatic, leadership expertise that for far too long has not been taught in our churches, Bible schools and seminaries.

This book is a treasure trove of biblical tools for anyone serious about elevating their level of strategic leadership skills, empowering them to engage victoriously in our battle with the kingdom of darkness.

Postlude                                                      183